Challenge to Community Psychiatry

COMMUNITY MENTAL HEALTH SERIES
Sheldon R. Roen, Ph.D., Editor

Community Psychology Series
General Editor: Daniel Adelson, Ph.D.

Research Contributions from Psychology to Community Mental Health
Edited by Jerry W. Carter, Jr., Ph.D.

Issues in Community Psychology and Preventive Mental Health
By The Task Force on Community Mental Health, Division 27 of the American Psychological Association

Challenge to Community Psychiatry
Edited by Archie R. Foley, M.D.

Coordinate Index Reference Guide to Community Mental Health
By Stuart E. Golann, Ph.D.

Critical Issues in Community Mental Health
Edited by Harry Gottesfeld, Ph.D.

The Mental Health Team in the Schools
By Margaret Morgan Lawrence, M.D.

The Ecology of Mental Disorders in Chicago
By Leo Levy, Ph.D. and Louis Rowitz, Ph.D.

Psychiatric Disorder and the Urban Environment
Edited by Berton H. Kaplan, Ph.D. In Collaboration with: Alexander H. Leighton, M.D., Jane M. Murphy, Ph.D., and Nicholas Freydberg, Ph.D.

The Therapeutic Community: A Sourcebook of Readings
Edited by Jean J. Rossi, Ph.D. and William J. Filstead

Mental Health and the Community: Problems, Programs, and Strategies
Edited by Milton F. Shore, Ph.D. and Fortune V. Mannino, Ph.D.

CHALLENGE TO COMMUNITY PSYCHIATRY

A Dialogue between Two Faculties

Edited by
Archie R. Foley, M.D.

With a Foreword by
Lawrence C. Kolb, M. D.

Behavioral Publications, **New York**
1972

Library of Congress Catalog Card Number 71-174266
Standard Book Number 87705-063-5
Copyright © 1972 by Behavioral Publications

BEHAVIORAL PUBLICATIONS, 2852 Broadway—Morningside Heights,
New York, New York 10025

Printed in the United States of America

CONTENTS

CHAPTER 1

Prologue   1
Archie R. Foley, M.D.

CHAPTER 2

**The Planning: Process and   18
    Participation**
Archie R. Foley, M.D., and
    H. Keith H. Brodie, M.D.

CHAPTER 3

The Institute: Content and Process   29
H. Keith H. Brodie, M.D., and Archie R.
    Foley, M.D.

CHAPTER 4

Reflections of the Faculty   55

FOREWORD

In a casual conversation with me many months before the Institute for Training in Community and Social Psychiatry was held in Boston, Dr. Bernard Bandler, then Chairman of the Division of Psychiatry of the Boston University School of Medicine, outlined an educational proposal he had been turning over in his mind. No sooner had he uttered a few sentences than I was aware that the faculty members of the Division of Community and Social Psychiatry of Columbia University with which I was associated might have the privilege of participating in a unique interchange—one between the faculties of two medical school departments confronted with a similar problem that challenges current educational theory and practice. The interchange would be concerned with the challenge to community psychiatry that has emerged so strongly in recent years. The force of that challenge was developed from the passage of the Federal Community Mental Health Act of 1963, an act that made available federal grant monies to communities to support the development of local services for persons who are mentally or emotionally disabled.

To be sure, many years before this federal legislation came into being psychiatrists had been preoccupied with and had initiated research to determine whether social factors might influence the occurrence of persistent disability due to psychiatric disorder. Other psychiatrists, as a result, undertook operational changes in service programs based on concepts that held social factors to be significant in the instigation and perpetuation of disability resulting from mental disease. From these early studies and experiments special training programs in community psychiatry and its administration have been developed.

The Columbia University Division of Community and Social Psychiatry was created to unite the interests of the Department of Psychiatry and the School of Public Health and Administrative Medicine of the College of Physicians and Surgeons. The division's faculty had completed a decade of slowly evolving experience in relation to commitment to psychiatric education and research focused upon the issues concerned with the provision of new and more effective psychiatric services in local communities. It was this experience, which had been accrued under the leadership of Dr. Viola W. Bernard, director of the division, that Dr. Bandler recognized as something that might be shared with his faculty at Boston University.

In many respects the teaching faculties of these two university departments of psychiatry hold similar values. They are both devoted to excellence in their educational programs for medical students and aspiring psychiatrists. They both desire that each trainee come to understand personality development in depth as a means of comprehending its distortions in psychopathology, and at both universities the resident psychiatrists gain this knowledge by observing and participating in the use of psychodynamic therapies. Such teaching and learning, which requires prolonged and intensive work with some of the ill, induces a degree of cautiousness and humility in one's expectations of what can be accomplished by simple manipulations of the external environment. This holds true whether the ill persons are hospitalized psychotic patients or are being treated through the psychosomatic services of a general hospital either as inpatients or outpatients.

This kind of learning, coupled with doubts regarding the capacity of existing faculty manpower to undertake new teaching responsibilities and concerns regarding changes in methods of service, has brought to the fore the anxieties in faculties when they are challenged to assume new responsibilities through the teaching and practice of community psychiatry. The hope of Drs. Bandler, Bernard, and Foley was that many of the sources of anxiety might be explored and that conflicts might be resolved by the sharing of experiences in a series of discussions among members of the two faculties. Hopefully, this account of the proceedings of the institute will enable other faculty groups the opportunity to share these experiences with regard to similar issues and conflicts in which they are involved.

It is my pleasure to express in behalf of the Columbia faculty our gratification for the opportunity to assist in planning the institute and to participate in it. As participants, we learned much through the discovery of problems similar to those our colleagues perceived or reported and through the frank, mutual exchanges in the small-group discussions. The interchange of experience with our colleagues in the Boston University Division of Psychiatry, we believe, will prove of mutual value as we undertake new ventures in community and social psychiatry.

Lawrence C. Kolb, M.D.

PREFACE

The following pages unfold a drama of several acts told in a dialogue between representatives of the faculties of two university departments of psychiatry. The cast of characters comprising the faculty of the Institute for Training in Community and Social Psychiatry held in Boston in June, 1968 was carefully selected on the basis of special expertise in that field. Each chapter of this book demonstrates, with varying emphasis, the roles, functions, and involvement of each participant in the institute.

Dr. Lawrence C. Kolb gave wholehearted support to this project from its inception. He provided the foreword to the institute, just as he has to these proceedings. The several chapters reflect not only the involvement of the participants but also their theoretical formulations and ideas regarding the practice of community psychiatry. They also present their candid, refreshing, not always congruous, and sometimes critical observations concerning the process of the institute.

The chapter entitled "The Planning: Process and Participation" tells of all that was involved in organizing the institute. Next, "The Institute: Content and Process" presents the processes within the institute and the content covered in each of the eight discussion groups and their deliberations over the four-day period. "Reflections of the Faculty" is just that: feelings and observations concerning the institute related with considerable candor by the discussion leaders. The faculty comments have been edited as little as possible because of their richness, the willingness of the discussion leaders to discuss conflictual material frankly, some sensitive interpersonal situations that developed, and the misgivings of these participants in the institute about their own roles and about the role of the institute itself. We are indebted to them both for their responses and their willingness to let us publish their comments almost verbatim. The chapter by Dr. Bernard Bandler, "The Aftermath: Faculty Process, Faculty Power, and Democracy," relates the changes—both organizational and structural—within the Boston University Division of Psychiatry that came about after the institute. "The Evaluation" deals with the efforts of Dr. Samuel W. Bloom and Dr. Sherman Eisenthal to determine the impact of the institute on the participants. Dr. Viola W. Bernard's chapter, "Commentary: Reflection on the Over-all Institute Experience," reveals some of her reflections on the process of the institute. They are especially noteworthy in view of her own deep involvement in all its phases.

As the editor of this book, I have had the opportunity to relive my own experience with the institute during the course of collecting and organizing the data on which this volume is based. This experience, at some distance and time from the pressures that prevailed during the institute itself, has given me a greater appreciation of its impact. I trust it will prove equally rewarding to the readers of this account and evaluation of the institute.

Archie R. Foley, M.D.

ACKNOWLEDGEMENTS

To all who assisted and participated in the institute and in the preparation of this publication, I wish to express my acknowledgment of their contributions and my gratitude for them.

Special thanks are due Dr. H. Keith H. Brodie, for his aid in organizing materials from the institute and in writing portions of the manuscript; Miss Coryl Jones, for her editorial assistance and serving as my adviser on the publication of this book; Dr. Stanley Hammons, for his case presentation to the participants on the evening preceding the institute; Mr. Joseph Devlin, Boston University Division of Psychiatry, for his efforts in coordinating the planning for the institute and the institute itself; Dr. James Mann, Boston University School of Medicine, for the role he played in the development and planning of the institute; Dr. David G. Satin, Boston University School of Medicine, for his help in organizing the efforts and material of the recorders—a service that was so vital to the success of the institute and to this account and evaluation of it; Miss Inge Hirschfeld, Executive Secretary, Columbia University Division of Community and Social Psychiatry, for her help during the entire planning process and during the institute itself; Miss Mary Laspada, Executive Secretary, Division of Psychiatry, Boston University School of Medicine; and the recorders of the institute, who were drawn from the list of participants and whose notes form the base for much of this document, since no formal papers were presented. Thanks are also extended to the secretarial staffs of the Boston University Division of Psychiatry and the Columbia University Division of Community and Social Psychiatry.

I would also like to thank the members of the secretarial staff of the Department of Psychiatry, Catholic Medical Center of Brooklyn and Queens, New York: Misses Linda Hickman and Valerie Paccione, for typing the manuscripts; and Miss Sylvia Maraia, for proofreading and assembling the contents.

Finally, those of us who have already benefited from the institute wish to make a special acknowledgment to the Continuing Education Program of the National Institute of Mental Health for the grant support that made possible the dialogue between the two faculties that is reported in this book.

Archie R. Foley, M.D.

THE INSTITUTE FACULTY*

THE PLANNING COMMITTEE:

Bernard Bandler, M.D., Professor of Psychiatry and Chairman, Division of Psychiatry, Boston University School of Medicine

Viola W. Bernard, M.D., Clinical Professor of Psychiatry and Director, Division of Community and Social Psychiatry, Columbia University

Archie R. Foley, M.D., Associate Clinical Professor of Psychiatry, Division of Community and Social Psychiatry, Columbia University

Samuel Bloom, Ph.D., Professor of Sociology in Community Medicine, Mount Sinai School of Medicine of the City University of New York

DISCUSSION LEADERS:

C. Knight Aldrich, M.D., Professor of Psychiatry, University of Chicago Medical School, Chicago, Illinois

Elizabeth B. Davis, M.D., Associate Professor of Psychiatry, Columbia University; Director, Department of Psychiatry, Harlem Hospital Center

Sheldon Gaylin, M.D., Assistant Clinical Professor of Psychiatry, Division of Community and Social Psychiatry, Columbia University

Natalie Goldart, M.S.W., Assistant Professor of Administrative Medicine (Psychiatric Social Work), School of Public Health and Administrative Medicine, Columbia University

Florence Liben, M.D., Associate in Psychiatry, Division of Community and Social Psychiatry, Columbia University

Louis Linn, M.D., Associate Clinical Professor of Psychiatry, Division of Community and Social Psychiatry, Columbia University

Alvin Mesnikoff, M.D., Associate Clinical Professor of Psychiatry, Columbia University

Marvin E. Perkins, M.D., Professor of Psychiatry, Mount Sinai School of Medicine of the City University of New York; Director of Psychiatry, Beth Israel Medical Center, New York City

RESOURCE CONSULTANTS:

Morton Bard, Ph.D., Professor of Psychology and Director, Psychology Center, City College, City University of New York

Viola W. Bernard, M.D., Clinical Professor and Director Division of Community and Social Psychiatry, Columbia University

Richard L. Blumenthal, Ph.D., Social Psychologist, Division of Community and Social Psychiatry, Columbia University

Camille Jeffers, Professional Assistant, Southeastern Educational Laboratory, Atlanta, Georgia

Ruth Newman, Ph.D., Professor, Department of Human Development, University of Maryland

xiv

Alex Richman, M.D., M.P.H., Associate Professor of Epidemiology, Division of Epidemiology, and Director, Psychiatric Epidemiology Training Program, Columbia University

Maurice V. Russell, M.S.W., Ed.D., Director of Social Service, Harlem Hospital; Associate Professor of Administrative Medicine, School of Public Health and Administrative Medicine, Columbia University

Leonard Siegel, M.D., Associate Attending Physician and Physician in Charge of Adolescent and Family Mental Health Services, Maimonides Medical Center, Brooklyn, New York

Kendon Smith, M.D., Associate in Psychiatry, Division of Community and Social Psychiatry, Columbia University

Leo Srole, Ph.D., Professor of Psychiatry (Social Sciences) and Chief, Psychiatric Research (Social Sciences), New York State Psychiatric Institute

Mervyn Susser, M.D., Professor and Head, Division of Epidemiology, School of Public Health and Administrative Medicine, Columbia University

* Titles are those held by the faculty members at the time of the Institute.

PARTICIPANTS IN THE INSTITUTE

* Juliette Anderson, R.N., Psychiatric Nurse, University Hospital, Boston

Mrs. Louise Bandler, M.S.W., Associate Professor of Psychiatric Social Work, Simmons School of Social Work, Boston

* Isaac L. Battin, Jr., M.D., Psychiatrist, Teaching Assistant, University Hospital, Boston

Claire E. Bent, M.S.W., Social Worker, Clinical Instructor in Psychiatry, Douglas A. Thom Clinic for Children, Boston

Leon R. Briggs, M.D., Psychiatrist, Associate in Psychiatry, Boston University-Boston City Hospital Child Guidance Clinic, Boston

Bernard Bruce, Ph.D., Psychologist, Relocation Study Center, University Hospital, Boston

Padriac Burns, M.D., Psychiatrist, Instructor in Psychiatry, Child Development Unit, Boston University

* Genevieve C. Carpenter, Ph.D., Psychologist, Assistant Research Professor of Psychology, Child Development Unit, University Hospital, Boston

* George H. Carter, M.D., Psychiatrist, Associate Professor of Psychiatry, University Hospital, Boston

* Lois Dellert, R.N., Psychiatric Nurse, University Hospital, Boston

Joseph Devlin, M.S.W., Social Worker, Community Coordinator, Boston University Mental Health Center Studies, Boston

James W. Dykens, M.D., Psychiatrist, Associate Clinical Professor of Psychiatry, Massachusetts Department of Mental Health, Boston

Sherman Eisenthal, Ph.D., Psychologist, Roxbury Multiservice Center, Roxbury

Seymour Fisher, M.D., Psychologist, Research Professor of Psychology, Director of Research Training Program, Boston University

Ellen Fitzgerald, Ph.D., Psychologist, Relocation Study Center, University Hospital, Boston

Harley Frank, Ph.D., Sociologist, University Hospital, Boston

Phillip H. Gates, M.D., Psychiatrist, Assistant Clinical Professor of Child Psychiatry, James Jackson Putnam Children's Center, Boston

* Ira Goldberg, Psychologist, Instructor in Psychiatry, Director, Relocation Study Center, University Hospital, Boston

Monroe Green, M.S.W., Social Worker, Director, South End Center for Alcoholics and Unattached Individuals, Boston

Kalman Heller, Ph.D., Psychologist, Worcester Youth Guidance Center, Worcester

Lester Houston, Social Worker, Director, Roxbury Comprehensive Health Center, Roxbury

Pierre Johannet, M.D., Psychiatrist, Assistant Clinical Professor of Psychiatry, Roxbury Comprehensive Health Center, Roxbury

Richard J. Kahn, M.D., Psychiatrist, Associate in Psychiatry, Boston University

Samuel Kaplan, M.D., Psychiatrist, Clinical Professor of Child Psychiatry, Associate Director of Child Psychiatry, Child Development Unit, University Hospital, Boston

Paul Kaufman, M.D., Psychiatrist, Associate in Psychiatry, Boston University Medical Center

* Ann Kilguss, Social Worker, Relocation Study Center, University Hospital, Boston

Peter H. Knapp, M.D., Psychiatrist, Research Director of Psychiatry, Boston University Medical Center

Marvin B. Krims, M.D., Psychiatrist, Assistant Clinical Professor of Psychiatry, Boston University-Boston City Hospital Child Guidance Center

Conan Kornetsky, Ph.D., Psychologist, Research Professor of Psychology, Psychopharmacology Research Laboratory, Boston University

Lois Lang, Social Worker, Boston University-Boston City Hospital Child Guidance Center

* Alan Lazerson, M.D., Psychiatrist, Associate in Psychiatry, Boston University

Patricia Lee, Social Worker, Relocation Study Center, University Hospital, Boston

Mildred McCarthy, M.S.S.W., Social Worker, Clinical Instructor in Child Psychiatry, James Jackson Putnam

Children's Center, Boston

* Douglas M. McNair, Ph.D., Psychologist, Associate Professor of Psychiatry, Psychopharmacology Research Laboratory, Boston University Medical Center

* Kathy McWey, R.N., Psychiatric Nurse, University Hospital, Boston

* Thomas Maier, M.D., Psychiatrist, Teaching Assistant in Psychiatry, University Hospital, Boston

William I. Malamud, Jr., M.D., Psychiatrist, Associate Professor of Psychiatry, Boston University

James Mann, M.D., Psychiatrist, Coordinator of Residency Training, Professor of Psychiatry, Boston University

* Joanne Meader, Social Worker, Boston University-Boston City University

Allan F. Mirsky, Ph.D., Psychologist, Professor of Neuropsychology, NIMH Research Investigator, Research Department, Boston University

Richard C. Morrill, M.D., Psychiatrist, Instructor in Psychiatry, Roxbury Comprehensive Health Center, Roxbury

Robert E. Moss, M.D., Psychiatrist, Boston

* James Muller, Ph.D., Psychologist, Head Psychologist, University Hospital, Boston

Arthur E. Mutter, M.D., Psychiatrist, Assistant Professor of Psychiatry, Clinical Director, Child Guidance Clinic, Boston University

John B. Nelson, III, M.D., Psychiatrist, Assistant Clinical Professor of Psychiatry, Director, Douglas A. Thom

Clinic for Children, Boston

S. Joseph Nemetz, M.D., Psychiatrist, Associate Professor of Psychiatry, Boston University

Ralph R. Notman, M.D., Associate Professor of Psychiatry, Boston University Mental Health Center Studies

Phyllis G. Oram, Ph.D., Psychologist, Assistant Research Professor of Psychiatry, Roxbury Multiservice Center, Roxbury

Richard Pillard, M.D., Psychiatrist, Instructor in Psychiatry, Boston University

Herbert I. Posin, M.D., Psychiatrist, Associate Clinical Professor of Psychiatry, Brandeis University, Waltham, Massachusetts

* Rebecca M. Reetz, Social Worker, Psychiatric Outpatient Department, University Hospital, Boston

Eveoleen N. Rexford, M.D., Psychiatrist, Professor of Child Psychiatry, Boston University

Catherine Roff, Ph.D., Psychologist, James Jackson Putnam Children's Center, Boston

Melvin Rosenthal, Ph.D., Psychologist, Associate Professor of Clinical Psychology, Head Psychologist, University Hospital, Boston

Lorraine Sahm, Sociologist, University Hospital, Boston

Louis W. Sander, M.D., Psychiatrist, Associate Research Professor of Psychiatry, Child Development Unit, Boston University

David G. Satin, M.D., Psychiatrist, Assistant Professor of Psychiatry, Psychopharmacology Research Laboratory, Boston University

Sebastine Santostefano, Ph.D., Psychologist, Associate Professor of Psychiatry, Boston University-Boston City Hospital Child Guidance Center

Evelyne Schwaber, M.D., Psychiatrist, Instructor in Psychiatry, Boston University-Boston City Hospital Child Guidance Center

Alice Schwartz, Social Worker, Psychiatric Outpatient Department, University Hospital, Boston

Roy M. Shulman, M.D., Psychiatrist, Instuctor of Psychiatry, Boston University, (Massachusetts Rehabilitation Commission, Roxbury)

James C. Skinner, M.D., Psychiatrist, Associate Professor of Psychiatry, University Hospital, Boston

Gerald Stechlet, Ph.D., Psychologist, Associate Research Professor of Psychology, Head Psychologist, Child Guidance Clinic, University Hospital, Boston

Nancy W. Stern, Ph.D., Psychologist, Clinical Instructor in Psychiatry (Psychology), Douglas A. Thom Clinic for Children, Boston

Evelyn Stiles, M.S.W., Social Worker, Psychiatric Outpatient Department, University Hospital, Boston

Jacob Swartz, M.D., Psychiatrist, Associate Professor of Psychiatry, Director, Outpatient Clinic, Boston University

Fred Tavil, M.D., Public Health Physician, Roxbury Comprehensive Health Center, Roxbury

* Louis Vachon, M.D., Psychiatrist, Assistant Professor of Psychiatry, Research Unit, Boston University

Suzanne T. Van Amerongen, M.D., Psychiatrist, Assistant Clinical Professor of Psychiatry, Douglas A. Thom Clinic for Children, Boston

Howard Weintraub, M.D., Psychiatrist, Assistant Clinical Professor of Psychiatry, Director of Training, Douglas A. Thom Clinic for Children, Boston

Jean Wirzburger, R.N., Psychiatric Nurse, University Hospital, Boston

Anna K. Wolff, M.D., Psychiatrist, Assistant Clinical Professor, Boston University-Boston City Hospital Child Guidance Clinic

Grace Young, Ph.D., Chief Psychologist, James Jackson Putnam Children's Center, Boston University

* Allyn Zanger, D.S.V., Social Worker, Assistant Professor of Psychiatry, Head Social Worker, Boston University-Boston City Hospital, Child Guidance Clinic

* Recorders in small group sessions

1. PROLOGUE

Archie R. Foley, M.D.

The Institute for Training in Community and Social Psychiatry that was held in Boston in June, 1968 was a dialogue between the faculties of the Division of Psychiatry, Boston University School of Medicine, and the Division of Community and Social Psychiatry of the Department of Psychiatry and the School of Public Health and Administrative Medicine, Columbia University. This involvement of one faculty in toto with another faculty in toto is quite unprecedented.

THE PLETHORA OF PRECURSORS

The precursors of this institute were many and varied. The format of this one, however, differed quite markedly from previous attempts to introduce concepts and content of community psychiatry into the curricula of medical schools, residency training programs in psychiatry, and the training programs of related professional disciplines.

The body of knowledge evolving from community and social psychiatry has been rapidly expanding during the past decade. A plethora of methods and processes has been developed to translate this knowledge into practical applications. Training programs, most of them subsidized by the National Institute of Mental Health, have sprung up in university medical centers throughout the country. They were directed first toward integrating the content of community psychiatry in residency programs, then toward augmenting more traditional training in post-residency programs. Now, because the psychiatrist is involved in planning, organizing, coordinating, imple-

1

menting, and evaluating comprehensive community mental health services, his training needs to be even broader so that he can handle the multifaceted roles he must play. Currently, there are approximately twenty specialized training programs, varying in size, duration, depth of study, and goals. A basic tenet of each, however, is that traditional training of the psychiatric resident does not equip him to work in or to direct comprehensive community-oriented mental health service programs, even though this is the major thrust and pattern of the delivery of psychiatric services today. Community psychiatrists are needed not only as staff members in the 250 or so community mental health centers now in operation but also as consultants, as directors of psychiatric services in general hospitals and many other settings, and, of course, as teachers and researchers in mental health and related fields.

In 1964, the National Institute of Mental Health sponsored four regional training institutes of four days each for chairmen of psychiatry departments and directors of psychiatric residency programs to stimulate the inclusion of content concerned with community mental health in their programs. In these sessions, papers dealing with theoretical considerations, program planning and content, and research methodology were presented and then discussed in small groups. Other papers stressed the need to recognize the relevance and importance of community psychiatry and to increase activities in community mental health. One result of these institutes was the organization of a series of NIMH-sponsored workshops for senior faculty members that have been conducted for two-week periods several times in the past few years. One program to extend the expertise of the experts, completed in 1967, consisted of a series of Visiting Faculty Seminars at the Laboratory of Community Psychiatry at Harvard University. This program was followed by an expansion of Harvard's instructional program in community psychiatry, including a program of continuing education and field work for psychiatrists on leave of absence from agencies and institutions.

By the fall of 1967, six other university departments of psychiatry—Chicago, Duke, Baylor, Pittsburgh, Vermont, and California-San Francisco—had inaugurated similar seminars for faculty and practitioners. Some schools, such as Columbia, had conducted programs in community psychiatry since 1956. An initial problem in education at this level is by whom and how the experts themselves are taught. Another issue is how the desire for continuing education can be instilled to such a degree that professionals will have the initiative to seek, develop, and operate programs in continuing education, inservice training, and consultative services. This problem lies at the core of curricular issues in medical schools, particularly in specialty programs. Two other questions also require examination: What conditions are necessary to make possible the flexibility to accept newly found information and to put it to use? What are the relationships among service, training, and research in this area?

The Southern Regional Education Board (SREB) conducted a conference in December, 1966 to explore the complex issues and problems medical schools encounter in planning a community mental health service as part of their teaching facilities.[1] The conference can be summarized by the charge to training programmers given by Dr. Morton Miller, a member of the staff of the National Institute of Mental Health: "Innovate or deteriorate." Issues arise as to how to get faculties to accept innovation without deterioration of faculty communication and the faculty community. Because of the innovativeness of community psychiatry, issues also emerge over problems of professional identity that are compounded by concerns over newness versus tradition.

A case in point is the evaluations trainees in the community mental health training program at Langley Porter Psychiatric Institute in San Francisco submitted regarding their experiences.[2] They commented unanimously that training field assignments were stressful and demanding and made them anxiously evaluate their roles. Each trainee also stated that the consultation experience prepared him for a role he anticipated would be a part of his practice. The training elements most frequently evaluated negatively were coursework and seminars. Most trainees generally visualized their orientation to the system of the community as having some application to their professional lives in whatever city or area they would practice, but they did not really know how it would be relevant. About the field work they seemed to say, "I don't know what I learned, but I learned it." This is really an attitudinal stance—open-ended, open-minded, and problem-oriented—that is crucial to community mental health. A psychiatrist might well respond to training in community psychiatry with comments similar to that of a predoctoral fellow in psychology assigned to San Francisco's Chinatown: "What I don't know about Chinatown could fill many volumes. The main thing I know firsthand is that it was hard for me to learn very much about Chinatown firsthand. . . ."[3] What he had learned, he then added, was to reassess his acceptance of commonly held stereotypes; to examine other sources and social indicators; and to trace successful and unsuccessful patterns of acculturation and transition for the Chinese as well as for other national ethnic groups. This is what the faculty member not concerned with community psychiatry needs to be able to accept from his colleagues in community psychiatry and, in the process, to benefit by.

NIMH SUPPORT OF CONTINUING EDUCATION

NIMH training-grant support for continuing education in mental health—as distinguished from community mental health center programs in consultation and education—was initiated in 1967 with a conference concerning continuing education as an agent of change. It formed the basis of the current NIMH program in this area. Representatives were brought in from industry, universities, community mental health programs, continuing education programs, mental health administration, and program planning and from local, state, and federal governments. Their conclusion was that education is more than formal training and must be continued throughout one's lifetime. Industry was cited for allocating private funds for its own continuing education needs, with the training undertaken wherever it is available according to the initiative of the individual. A follow-through conference in April, 1969 focused on problems encountered by persons in state and regional programs in relating to continuing education.

NIMH has supported programs in continuing education irrespective of generalization or specialization in medical practice or of the research, training, or community setting. Its objective has been the effective utilization of all service resources, the currency of information and procedures used in medical-mental health settings, and the implementation of more effective patterns of service. NIMH has given priority to strengthening continuing education in training centers for mental health practitioners and teachers; to implementing community and state efforts in mental health planning and programming; and to meeting the needs of target groups of recipients, as contrasted to offering isolated courses for whoever may be recruited. Many of these projects have been workshops and conferences conducted by organizations such as the American Academy of General Practice, the Western Interstate Commission for Higher Education, and the Southern Regional Education Board. Other projects have included courses such as those listed by the American Medical Association.

To further the development of continuing education programs, NIMH published a series of annotated bibliographies on inservice training and methods.[4] Such material is rich in information and sources but scant in references to actual continuing education programs, especially those for community mental health. Of special note are the types of possible educational programs, ranging from in-basket games to role-playing and sensitivity training, plus the more sedate case method, conference modes, and seminar series. One clearly indicated factor is the appropriateness of method to problem and resource.

The Western Interstate Commission for Higher Education (WICHE), a public agency that works across state lines to improve education and to administer the Western Regional Educational Compact adopted by thirteen states, entered the mental health field to develop manpower for direct and indirect services. WICHE's projects for continuing education range from special programs for psychiatric education for physicians remote from teaching centers to evaluations of training programs.[5] WICHE aims to increase the number of psychiatrist-teachers to serve general practitioners. It has sponsored such activities as visitation programs—one to a comprehensive rural mental health service in New Mexico and another to psychiatric emergency services in Los Angeles; regional conferences on preventive services in mental health; and the publication and distribution of materials on mental health problems, program evaluation conference proceedings, behavioral science research for mental health, surveys of various types, and the like. The western states are forced to be innovative by their need to make optimal use of their resources and to develop new ones. When compared to those in areas richer in mental health resources, their activities illustrate a paradox: the inverse ratio between resources and innovation. Many of the major medical training centers are high on resources. The reader can draw his own conclusion as to their receptivity to innovation.

Other examples of continuing education can be cited: the Associated Faculties Program in Community Psychiatry of the Washington School of Psychiatry; models using consultants, such as the training program for child development consultants at George Peabody College for Teachers in Nashville, with its seminar-practicum-internship; the continuing education program for psychiatrists in Houston, which started in the private homes of faculty members of Baylor University and brought town and gown together with invited guests; and the myriad of possibilities with field visits and the bringing in of practitioners to the training setting.

Small-scale but workable collaboration results from all the multidisciplinary and interagency appointment programs, such as joint appointments by universities,

agencies, and hospitals and arrangements for private practitioners. Any joint or participatory program can be educational and comprehensive, especially if it is focused on problem-solving techniques, field and/or case work, consultants, involvement of advisory groups, resource inventory orientation tours and exchange visit programs, "preceptorships" in community mental health and related service agencies, and consultation programs with individual consultees. Each has been used to some extent in numerous situations throughout the country, but the lack of concerted effort has greatly reduced their impact, perhaps even negated it. Motivations of the training recipients frequently are suspect, and the long-term benefits certainly are.

Over the years, the psychiatric profession has attempted in many ways to evolve meaningful training programs, but didactic presentations have tended to be erudite and case presentations have their limitations. In terms of providing meaningful training experiences, the message is clear: the training must be provided within an operational framework, problem-solving-oriented, and practical; in addition, it must be ongoing, to develop relationships for meaningful exchanges, and must contribute both information and an appropriate attitude toward its use.

It deserves repeating that innovative training techniques must be implemented in medical schools, residency programs, and the professional medical community; at the level of the student, the faculty, and the practitioner; and among the fractions of each of these. Training must take into account that comprehensive health and mental health care needs to take place on many levels—not only in the provision of services but also in the development of new techniques for training health professionals in the delivery of services and in the refinement of research techniques to measure their effectiveness. The recent trends in community mental health toward services based on the three public health levels of prevention—primary, secondary, and tertiary—emphasize preventive measures and rehabilitative services encompassing a wide variety of approaches to enhance interpersonal skills and social and vocational retraining. These new directions augment the more limited approaches of treating the patient when his disorder has developed to the extent that his level of functioning emotionally, socially, and occupationally has been impaired.

The 1967 amendments to the Community Mental Health Centers Act, extending time and funds to let communities deploy their resources to augment comprehensive services, have signified that organizational patterns for services are changing and that the basic medical model, rather than being supplanted, is being augmented to include all relevant health, sociological, and environmental services needed for successful intervention to improve the living conditions of the entire population.

This impetus to new services and extensions into comprehensive health services can be illustrated by the fact that 40 per cent of the community mental health center projects offer new consultative services and that another 40 per cent have broadened both the types and extent of consultation offered by their initial mental health service. The manpower needs to provide such services are, of course, demanding. To meet these needs, new types of personnel must be trained and existing skills must be augmented through inservice and continuing education of professionals. A complementary need is training medical school faculties. Herein lies another part of the problem. Courses in psychiatry, albeit short-term ones, are available. Not available, however, are courses and programs of inservice training and continuing education in community psychiatry. The subject matter of community psychiatry presents problems because it requires an understanding of the underlying social and behavioral sciences as well as the medical ones.

SPECIAL TRAINING IN
MENTAL HEALTH ADMINISTRATION

What is needed for the administration of the amalgam called comprehensive mental health services, and what is available for this demanding field? Although courses in administration are being emphasized in several training institutions, few stress the special demands of mental health administration. Special training is needed in regular residency training programs, in post-residency programs, in state departments of mental health, and in other institutional settings. One program, "The Mental Health Centers Operations Training Course," offered by the Department of Psychiatry and School of Public Health of the University of North Carolina in collaboration with agencies in neighboring states, is designed to enhance the administrative skills of persons from various state agencies responsible for mental health programming. A similar program is offered for professional staff of the State Department of Mental Hygiene in Ohio. A different perspective is being considered by the American Psychiatric Association. APA is exploring the feasibility of providing a fellowship, a type of fourth-year residency in Washington, D.C., that would emphasize administration, program planning, and experiences aimed at gaining a familiarity with federal agencies that have mental health components within their over-all programs, even though they are not primarily mental health agencies.

Various professional organizations also recognize the need to provide educational opportunities for their members. The American Psychiatric Association has developed a self-assessment protocol for psychiatrists as a form of continuing education. One-third of the total protocol is devoted to issues in administration and social and community psychiatry. After much deliberation and considerable controversy, the American Psychoanalytic Association has established a standing committee on community psychiatry.[6] It was set up on recommendations to the Council of the Association from its Standing Committee on Social Problems and from the New York Psychoanalytic Society, which urged the association to "adopt a statement expressing its positive support for the aims of community and social psychiatry and encouraging its members to participate appropriately in the development and implementation of research, sound programs, and well-founded principles in this complex and far-reaching field." The American Academy of Psychoanalysts issued a statement[7] pertaining to the role of the psychoanalyst in community mental health in which he was encouraged to involve himself in community mental health within his area of expertise.

Dr. Bernard Bandler recognized that, because of the disparities between traditional psychoanalytic and psychiatric orientations and the community psychiatric orientation, certain attitudes held and training techniques used by supervisors and senior faculty members in psychiatric residency training programs could be inimical to the training of psychiatric residents. He and others had become aware of the polarization developing in many training centers between persons committed to one or another of the approaches to mental disorders. At the same time that the resident was being encouraged to broaden his experience through community activities and consultation to community agencies and to become more aware of social conditions and cultural factors related to the occurrence of mental disorders, he was being supervised, all too frequently, by traditionally trained psychoanalysts who had given and continue to give major emphasis to intrapsychic phenomena and one-to-one therapy, often with little consideration for social and environmental factors as contributing factors to mental disturbance. Dr. Bandler and others felt that many of the more traditionally oriented psychiatrists and psychoanalysts lacked the flexibility necessary to work productively with communities to evolve mental health services based on their own needs.

When the Division of Psychiatry of the Boston University School of Medicine had to face up to its involvement in developing a community mental health center in Boston, such factors as the impact of faculty polarization, the inflexibility it can produce, and the impetus to resolve problems stemming from such entrenchments were all brought to a focus and helped set the stage for the institute discussed in this book. For Boston University to provide services in the community meant facing the reality of community action versus reaction—both of the faculty community and the catchment-area community—and facing the issue of separation versus integration of training, service, and research. Because of the need for faculty communication and education, their level of resources could not meet it—precisely because of the high degree of specialization, factionalization, and diversity that was required. To act, to communicate, to co-educate, to cooperate led them to innovate in the form of an experiment in faculty education.

THE PROPOSAL TO NIMH

In his application to NIMH for the grant it provided in support of the institute, Dr. Bandler said:

> The development of community mental health is probably the single most important development in psychiatry both at the present time and for the next decade. This development not only includes all the new centers that are being planned, but the evolution of many current facilities, such as state hospitals, clinics, general hospitals, and university centers, into community mental health centers. There is and increasingly will be need for enormous manpower to staff them. The adequacy of [existing] training programs is central to the preparation of psychiatric personnel to meet the responsibilities inherent in community mental health. There will be need for modifications and changes in current basic training programs as well as the development of advanced programs. Such changes are already taking place in many training centers. A program, however, is no stronger than its faculty. Most of the current faculty throughout the country are more prepared to train in the framework of traditional programs. A crucial problem for training, then, is faculty education in community mental health.
>
> The perspective of community psychiatry involves every person on the faculty, whatever his specific area of responsibility and functioning. The understanding, point of view, and attitude of each faculty member toward community psychiatry affect each resident and contribute toward the climate in which the resident learns and develops—a climate with an atmosphere of mutual respect in a group which shares a certain baseline of knowledge and common perspectives. This is not to advocate the slavish adherence to uniformity of ideas—scientific disagreements and efforts to resolve them through research are the lifeblood of any educational institution. But in a training institution that is basically split with respect to community mental health to the extent that the residents are caught in a cross-

fire, a similar split may occur among the residents themselves. Such an atmosphere militates against learning and
against a dispassionate inquiry into problems. . . . Faculty
polarization [is a very real danger] and of possibly crucial
importance in the development of training programs for
community mental health.

Community psychiatry imposes a new task for psychiatry and for the other mental health professions,
namely, the assumption of responsibility for the mental
health of a geographical area of the community. This responsibility implies the extension of the concept of the psychiatrist, a redefinition of his role, the acquisition of new
knowledge, and the development of new techniques. It
poses an opportunity, a challenge, and a threat to the
identity of the psychiatrist and to all mental health professionals. A defensive reaction by the traditional psychiatrist can lead to the disparagement of community psychiatry buttressed by the arguments that it involves him in
tasks beyond his professional competency and with the responsibilities beyond current knowledge and practice. He
can argue that residency training will be diluted and that
the psychiatrist will no longer have the expertness which
gives him professional identity. Such polarities are typical
of many faculties throughout the country.

These polarities state problems. They can be resolved.
Their resolution, however, implies an enlargement of
identity not only in an individual but in a group.[8]

RESOLUTION OF POLARIZATION PROBLEMS

The question was how these polarization problems
could be resolved and how a faculty could enlarge its
knowledge and integrate into its perspective the
viewpoint of community mental health. One way would
be to use clinical problems relevant to their natural
setting. The child psychiatrist and trainee in child psychiatry, for example, would find it difficult not to be
involved with schools, courts, settlement houses, social
agencies, consultation, and the like. Another way would
be through reading and discussion, faculty meetings,
and the speakers at Grand Rounds who contribute to
faculty discussions and education. Still another way
would be concerted activity in developing specific community mental health service programs in which many
individuals become involved in planning, thus bringing
them into relationship with community organizations.
Under such conditions, faculty and trainees serve as con-

sultants to community boards, neighborhood center staff, and others and work with local residents. These methods and experience would help, but they are not enough. They lack intensity, depth, and the concentrated time necessary to saturate one's self in the subject.

Textbooks on community psychiatry and regional workshops for professors of psychiatry do not give members of the faculty who actually work together an opportunity to subject their questions, doubts, uncertainties, and outright opposition to mutual examination and solution with experts. At such meetings, they face either other colleagues of like orientation or dissident faculty members from other training programs with whom they do not have to work daily. In work settings, they camouflage doubts to instill a sense of confidence in the recipient. A well-conceived plan of faculty education in community psychiatry must not only include the wealth of factual information that is already available but recognize fully the needs of a group of professionals who are, by tradition, independent; who tend generally to move slowly in new directions; and most important, who are themselves a community.

In his grant proposal to NIMH, Dr. Bandler also said:

> As a community, [the faculty] will tend to resist certain intrusions actively, some passively; it will silently engulf other intrusions and make them more like itself. It will move most appropriately when it is aware of its response to the need for change, especially when the changes contemplated need thorough clarification.
>
> The question then may be properly raised whether it would not be more helpful and useful to conduct intensive faculty education by employing a method that regards the faculty as a community in itself. From this point of view a four-day workshop may prove to be the most instructive tool for sharpening the appreciation of the faculty in respect to community psychiatry by noting and sharing the awareness of the various ways in which the faculty responds.... A workshop provides for the faculty to obtain expert, factual, and clinical information while at the same time having the opportunity to question, agree, and disagree. . . . The intensiveness of the work and the constant intimacy of the surrounds [of a workshop could] clarify, to a great extent, sources of concern and anxiety which [otherwise] would eventually exert their negative effects in hidden ways upon the future community

program and training, including polarization as a major manifestation.[9]

Such a workshop could be organized in any of several ways. Workshop leaders could represent different points of view in community psychiatry and focus on the major theoretical issues and on the realms of controversy. Or, leaders could be brought in from across the country solely because of their eminence in their respective fields. Or, a workshop could be organized by a group of individuals who had worked together and who had developed a body of experience in an urban community similar to the group seeking the experience and awareness to resolve its own educational problems. In this option, other participants could be brought in to supplement the experience of the invited group and to serve as additional resource personnel. This last alternative was the one chosen for the Boston University—Columbia University experiment in faculty education.

This experiment was designed as a participatory process for planning, conducting, and recording both the processes and the content of a four-day institute in Boston at which the faculties of the two universities would face each other to teach, to learn, and to share their experiences. The discussions of the experiences of the Columbia faculty would serve as a laboratory from which generalizations would emerge. All major topics would be covered via the problem-oriented method with the topics organized to cover service, training, and research. Participants (the Boston University faculty) would be divided into small discussion groups, each chaired by a member of the Columbia University group as a discussion leader with a recorder selected from the Boston group to winnow out the major questions that emerged from each session and that would then be presented at plenary sessions. A social scientist would make process studies and conduct an evaluation. From this point of development, a Planning Committee would work out the detailed organization and agenda.

POTENTIAL INSTITUTE RESULTS

Such an institute, as a form of inservice training for faculty, had the potential to produce results of significance far exceeding the educational benefits to the faculty participants involved. First, it could show that faculty education could achieve a common baseline of understanding and a unity of perspective regarding the scope and significance of community psychiatry as an essential component of resident training, perhaps thus healing or preventing faculty polarization. Second, it could provide a model for faculty education in general. Third, its approach to major topics via problem orientation and case demonstration, supplemented by the expertise of resource personnel responding to questions, could be evaluated as a workshop method. Lastly, the publication resulting from the institute could provide material of value to psychiatric education and to mental health educators such as social workers, nurses, psychologists, and social scientists. In short, its potential significance was great.

The potential for such an institute included several "sleepers" that awoke the authors and a number of others. These included the institute method as an educational process for institutional change, participatory processes in developing curricula, and certain attitudinal changes on the part of some institute participants toward concepts and the practice of community psychiatry.

The educational momentum of the institute, as evaluated from different perspectives at three different times—during, immediately after, and one year after the institute—turned out to be a classic "sleeper." The proposers anticipated an immediate impact because of the intensity of exchange sought at the institute, and they anticipated a gradual disbursement of influence. Instead, during and immediately after the institute, the personal stance of each participant remained unchanged to any observer or to any other participant. This was an unfortunate fact for the institute faculty to accept after all the expenditure of effort and the need not only to face the results of their own evaluation and to present negative results to the sponsor, NIMH, but to publish the results. However—and this is the real "sleeper"—the radiations from the experience for each participant proved to be cumulative over time, with subtleties and new working relationships revealing themselves after the incorporation of the experience into the organization and structure of the two faculties. Thanks to the work overload and the inevitable publication delays, the total process, content, and evaluation can now be presented over a period of time that makes them more meaningful because of the changes in scale and the time factor of the evaluation.

In an era of academic unrest and change, the participatory and planning process of the institute in Boston is offered as a successful model for education and attitudinal change. The dialogue between the Boston University and Columbia University psychiatric faculties that took place at the institute was a process of teachers teaching teachers and of the teaching teachers being taught.

REFERENCE NOTES

1. *The Medical School and the Community Mental Health Center,* Workshop Proceedings, Southern Regional Education Board. PHS Pub. No. 1858, 1967, Superintendent of Documents, Government Printing Office, Washington, D.C. 20402.

2. M. Robert Harris, Betty L. Kalis, and Lida Schneider, "Training for Community Mental Health in an Urban Setting," *American Journal of Psychiatry,* Supplement on Community Psychiatry, 124:4, 1967.

3. Ibid.

4. *Training Methodology. Part I: Background Theory and Research; Part II: Planning and Administration; Part III: Instructional Methods and Techniques (Revised); Part IV: Audiovisual Theory, Aids, and Equipment.* PHS Pub. No. 1862, 1969, Superintendent of Documents, Government Printing Office, Washington, D.C. 20402.

5. *The 1967 Annual Report of the Western Interstate Commission for Higher Education,* University East Campus, Boulder, Colorado, 1968.

6. Viola W. Bernard, M.D., chairman, Bernard Bandler, M.D., Elizabeth W. Davis, M.D., Louis Linn, M.D. (all of whom participated in the Boston institute), Jules V. Coleman, M.D., Reginald Lourie, M.D., Judd Marmor, M.D., Fritz Redl, Ph.D., S. Mouchly Small, M.D., and Albert J. Solnit, M.D. All are psychoanalysts involved in some aspects of community and social psychiatry.

7. Prepared by Margaret Morgan Lawrence, M.D., Victor F. Lief, M.D., and John A. P. Millet, M.D.

8. Bernard Bandler, "The Need for Faculty Education in Training Facilities," from "Workshop—Faculty Education in Community Psychiatry," NIMH Grant Application No. MH-9540-01, August, 1967, pp. 13–14.

9. Ibid., p. 15.

2. THE PLANNING: PROCESS AND PARTICIPATION

Archie R. Foley, M.D.
H. Keith H. Brodie, M.D.

The planning phase of the institute extended over a period of many months. Indeed, if the period of time from Dr. Bandler's initial conceptualization of the institute to its actual implementation is considered, a span of two years was involved. The level of activity varied from relative inactivity to impetuosity.

The concept of the institute included a method for participatory educational process; thus, communication among the members of the Planning Committee, participants, and institute faculty was cybernetic. Communication among members of the Planning Committee (Drs. Bandler, Bernard, Foley, and Bloom) was informal until a sufficient number of issues surfaced to merit collective decision-making; then, the members met to formalize issues and make decisions.

Before the application for support of the institution was submitted to NIMH, Samuel W. Bloom, Ph.D., then Professor of Sociology in Psychiatry, State University of New York, Downstate Medical Center, had agreed to participate as a social scientist to evaluate the institute process and content. Dr. Bloom served on the Planning Committee so that he could be in a position to relate the over-all process to the process of the institute and its impact on the participants and faculty. He developed the questionnaires and format to obtain data on the topics for discussion in the institute sessions and assisted in working out the over-all format of the institute.

Even though the proposal to NIMH included names, dates, and places of all persons who had verbally

consented to participate, much remained for fundamental planning by the committee. Such issues as
whether the institute should be held in Boston or some
place more neutral to the participants from Boston University had to be reduced to working details. The
consensus was that a site away from Boston would
provide an atmosphere more conducive to free interchange on a variety of levels, including professional and
social, than a place in Boston where participants would
be subject to the multiple distractions of professional,
social, and family responsibilities. However, the budget
dictated the decision that the institute be held in Boston.
This represented a difference of bringing over fifty
Bostonians to the vicinity of New York or sending fifteen
or more New Yorkers and others to Boston.

The decision that no formal papers would be presented
was made to reinforce the concept of a dialogue within
and between the two faculties. Barring formal papers
would provide the Boston faculty with more opportunities
to obtain needed relevant information as well as to
question, discuss, agree and disagree, and share feelings,
pro and con, about community psychiatry with the
institute faculty. Also, no time would be lost to ritual and
formality.

A key question concerned the ratio and number of
faculty members from Columbia University needed for a
working nucleus at the institute. Its success would hinge
largely on having a faculty of persons who had worked
together previously within a conceptual framework that
they had found acceptable as a group, recognizing
individual differences and varying points of view. As it
turned out, seven of the eleven resource consultants and
six of the eight discussion leaders came from Columbia
University; the rest were invited from seven other
training, service, and research organizations.

The role in the institute of the planners themselves
was an issue. Were they to be arbiters? Would they be
too busy in operating the institute to participate actively
in the deliberations? As chairmen and directors, were
they too much "the Establishment"? It was eventually
decided that Drs. Bernard and Foley of Columbia

University would assume primary responsibility for rounding out the institute faculty because of their expertise, experience, and knowledge of all the individuals involved and their willingness to assume the added work.

The planning agenda consisted of several interlocking phases and activities: polling Boston University participants regarding topics; matching topics and issues to resources; inviting faculty members to the institute and inviting the faculty for the institute; matching personal and professional dynamics in composing the groups; cumulative communication and scheduling; distributing introductory information that first had to be gathered from the resource consultants; all the minutiae of liaison for over seventy already busy faculty and the adjustments necessary when this number grew to around 100 by the time of the institute; and getting them all together in one place for the educational experience.

SELECTION OF INSTITUTE PARTICIPANTS

The first step was selecting and inviting the participants and finding out exactly what they felt they needed to have discussed—a crucial aspect of the problem-solution orientation of the institute and the participatory planning process concept. Originally, the institute was planned for forty-four participants from the Boston University faculty in the Division of Psychiatry, many of whom were directly involved in developing the program for the University's community mental health center in Boston. Letters of invitation as participants in the institute, however, were sent to fifty-four mental health professionals on the faculty of the Boston University School of Medicine, including thirty-two psychiatrists, eleven psychologists, seven social workers, and four nurses. This letter, signed by Drs. Bernard and Foley, requested each person to submit questions and issues he wished to have discussed. See Appendix, A, "Initial Letter to Participants." Of the fifty-four participants polled, forty-one returned letters with a total of 132 questions for discussion. These questions fell into fifteen categories:

(1) Definitions, roles, and history of community psychiatry
(2) Community psychiatry program planning
(3) Treatment modalities used in community psychiatry
(4) Mental health services to poverty areas
(5) Use of nonpsychiatric personnel
(6) Consultation
(7) Approaches to racial issues
(8) Some hazards and safeguards of community psychiatry
(9) Preventive and rehabilitative aspects of community psychiatry
(10) Pediatric community psychiatry
(11) Training in community psychiatry
(12) The neighborhood and the community
(13) Community mental health centers
(14) The future and goals of community psychiatry
(15) Research and evaluation

Based on this list of topics, the search was begun for resource consultants who could both cover the topics and interact meaningfully with the participants under the conditions anticipated for the institute.

SELECTION OF RESOURCE CONSULTANTS AND DISCUSSION LEADERS

The selection of resource consultants was a painstaking and time-consuming task. First, each had to be recruited verbally and informed about the goals and objectives of the institute—no easy matter because of the double-loaded professional-personal mix underlying the institute and the role the consultant would have to play in the small, intense group discussion sessions. After this contact to work out the content, process, and topical assignments with each consultant, he was sent a letter explaining the over-all plan, timeable, and assignments of the other faculty members. (See Appendix A, "Letter to Institute Faculty.")

The fifteen topics to be discussed, when matched to the corresponding expertise of the resource consultants, resulted in eight general areas of discussion. The following is the resulting assignments:

Bard:	Role of the consultant in developing training programs in existing community institutions (combining topics 5 and 6, use of non-psychiatric personnel and consultation)
Bernard/Smith:*	Training in community psychiatry and child community psychiatry (combining topics 2, 10, and 11, program planning, child psychiatry, and training in community psychiatry)
Blumenthal/Srole:**	Research and evaluation (topics 1 and 15 and overlap in all areas)
Newman:	Mental health services to poverty areas (topic 4) and rehabilitative aspects of community psychiatry (topic 9)
Russell:	Approaches to racial issues (topic 7), the neighborhood and the community (topic 12), and combining these for hazards and safeguards of community psychiatry (topic 8)
Siegel:	Innovative treatment approaches in community child psychiatry (combining topics 3 and 10, treatment modalities and child psychiatry in community psychiatry)

* Drs. Bernard and Smith substituted for Dr. Sally Provence, who at the last minute had to withdraw because of unforseen circumstances.
    ** Drs. Blumenthal and Srole and Drs. Susser and Richman also worked as teams of resource persons. Such an arrangement was predicated on the inability of each of the four persons to be at the institute for the entire period.

Susser/Richman.**   Research and evaluation (topic 15) and community psychiatry program planning (topic 2), which together covered the Community Mental Health Center and the future and goals of community psychiatry (topics 13 and 14)

Jeffers: Approaches to racial issues (topic 7) and child community psychiatry (topic 10), especially services in poverty areas (topic 4)

Each assignment would also include definitions, roles, and history (topic 1); hazards and safeguards (topic 8); community mental health centers (topic 13); and future goals of community psychiatry (topic 14).

The other component of the institute faculty, the discussion leaders, was to consist of Columbia University faculty members. The final roster, however, included six from Columbia and two other persons who had had close working experience with the Columbia group. The discussion leaders were to chair the small-group sessions and draw upon their own experience in community psychiatry in developing the topical discussions. These sessions would thus be problem-oriented, based on clinical demonstrations in community psychiatry in which the experiences of the Columbia and supplementary faculty served to catalyze discussions designed to clarify issues.

Each resource consultant and discussion leader was asked to submit two articles he considered relevant to his special area. This material was compiled as a list of recommended readings. (See Appendix B, "Recommended Readings.") To assure that each participant would be able to obtain the material for use as an introduction to the institute and have time to study it prior to the institute, some of the material was circulated to the participants in advance. The reading list was limited so that it would not overwhelm the participants even before they had a chance to get started. A curriculum vitae of each resource consultant and discussion leader was also sent to the participants to inform them about the special interests and experience of the consultants and discussion leaders.

By the time of the institute, the number of participants had grown to eighty-two. The Planning Committee divided this group into eight groups, each having a proportional representation of the various mental health professions. The average group included four psychiatrists, three psychologists, two social workers, and one nurse. Each of the intramural and extramural programs at Boston University was likewise represented throughout the eight groups; also, faculty who had worked together or had had responsibility for developing any particular program at Boston University—these frequently being senior faculty—were appointed throughout the groups. Members of various Boston University programs such as community psychiatry, research, or training were likewise dispersed. In addition, since the internal dynamics of the groups were as crucial as the mix, each group was composed with an eye toward each participant's capacity to integrate conceptual and experiential content, at least according to the estimates of the Planning Committee making the decisions. In other words, each group contained representation from each Boston University program for service, research, and training, each intra- and extramural program, each specialty field, each discipline, and each operational unit. This representation-separation was overlaid with a matching of conceptual-experiential makeup of the individuals in each group.

A discussion leader was then selected for each group—a person who the committee felt had the ability to deal constructively with the disparate viewpoints and negative attitudes toward community psychiatry known to be held by some of the participants assigned to his group. The discussion leader was to remain with his group for all eight of the institute sessions. The eight resource consultants were to rotate in a set sequence and to spend one three-hour session with each group. Special care was given to the assignments of resource consultants to groups for the first session since it was likely to set the tone for the operational framework for the remainder of the institute. Assignments were made after reviewing both the match between resource consultant and discussion leader and the composition of the group.

In all, each group would meet eight times. Each time it would have the same discussion leader but a different resource consultant, to allow for the discussion of different topics. Each session would last three hours, with a twenty minute coffee break each morning and afternoon.

To apprise the participants of the arrangements and results of the survey of topics, each was sent a letter confirming some arrangements and asking for his vote on others. (See Appendix A, "Second Letter to Participants.") One of the questions concerned holding evening meetings, which were vetoed later. The final schedule thus consisted of a total of eight daytime sessions, Monday through Thursday, June 9 to 13, 1968. There would be no formal papers, introductory material had already been circulated, and the meeting was to be held in Boston in a hotel familiar to most participants that was considered an appropriate setting for the desired kind of communication. The sessions would not be taped.

Other questions arose for the Planning Committee. How could its members obtain a feedback of information about what went on in the sessions, both to evaluate them and the institute as a whole and, if necessary to change directions and dynamics in midstream? At most workshops and professional meetings, the stage is set and however the play runs, that is the way it goes until the end; then, to find out what happened, one has to read the reviews. It is just such arrangements that have proved unsuccessful in education because once the participant is functioning within the process, he becomes powerless to change its course and has the options of dropping out by turning off the input, diverting the exchange to another topic or purpose, turning cynical, or extricating himself from the scene altogether. In anticipation of these problems of opting out or other forms of undeserved reactions and to offset their consequences, various special arrangements were made.

To get information about the sessions and feedback for

in-session modifications, Dr. Bandler designated two members from each discussion group as recorders to take extensive notes of what was discussed during each three-hour session. The recorders were instructed to note the group process and to record the sessions in terms of issues and actual content rather than to take general topic-outline notes. After each three-hour session, the recorder of each group was to dictate his notes into a dictaphone provided for this purpose. After each afternoon session, the recorders were to meet as a group with Dr. Foley of the Planning Committee to discuss the events of the day. Notes would be taken of these meetings, and each recorder would report to his group about activities in the other groups. The recorders' notes from these meetings were to report variations in group process and discussion content so that the persons attending the sessions could be apprised of the needs expressed in any one of the groups. Action could also be taken to modify the meeting structure before the next group discussion began the following morning.

The discussion leaders and resource consultants would meet daily as a group with Dr. Bernard so that the institute faculty could exchange information and impressions—a level of communication almost universally missing at workshops because each group and its faculty are operationally isolated from the others. These meetings would provide a vehicle for continuing input via the faculty and would inform them of issues raised in other groups and whether polarizations were being developed or diminished. The meetings would also indicate whether it was necessary to alter the approaches utilized by either the discussion leaders or the resource consultants for subsequent group meetings. These institute faculty meetings would also take place after the afternoon session while the recorders held their group meeting.

In addition, the Planning Committee—Drs. Bandler, Bernard, Foley, and Bloom—having visited the groups during the morning sessions, would meet each day at noon, to discuss and evaluate the progress of the institute in order to keep abreast of current developments and to intervene appropriately on the basis of the most recent developments in the groups.

A pre-institute meeting of the Planning Committee, resource consultants, discussion leaders, and other invitees, some of whom came from distant places, was held two weeks before the institute so that they could exchange views and become familiar with its over-all design. This meeting served to get the institute faculty in tune with its proposed dynamics. Everything was set and ready except for the introductory get-together of participants and faculty so that they could become sufficiently acquainted to get the institute started appropriately.

Of questionable value was the introductory session the Sunday evening before the first morning session. The Planning Committee "brought its own ants to the picnic," but in retrospect, the ants may have been little more than the differences and anxieties that had produced the idea and need for the institute in the first place.

A case presentation was selected to focus the attention of the audience for the subsequent group sessions. It concerned a patient whose therapy involved many of the basic principles of community psychiatry. The presentation included case material and videotape recordings by members of the Columbia University faculty. The consensus of the institute faculty and participants was that the presentation was unfortunate since it served as a vehicle for the expression of each participant's negative feelings about both the treatment of the patient and community psychiatry in general. This circumstance can be rationalized pro and con: that it brought out the issues that were the reason for the institute, or that it started the sessions with a negative orientation. In any case, the presentation elicited many suggestions that might have produced a more meaningful introduction. The reader is referred to Chapter four, "Reflections of the Faculty," for some of their comments in this regard.

This introductory session brought the two faculties together for a social interchange so that they could realign themselves as institute faculty and participants. They were seated randomly for dinner at tables for twelve. Dr. Bandler, as Chairman of the Boston University Division of Psychiatry, opened the after-dinner program. He introduced Dr. Lawrence C. Kolb of Columbia University, who discussed the significance of the institute and the perspective it represented. Dr. Bernard then discussed some of the salient issues, conceptual and operational, of community and social psychiatry; introduced the faculty of the institute; and outlined the program for the following four days. This evening meeting, except for the final evaluation session, was the only plenary session of all faculty and participants.

The institute then proceeded to go on its own cybernetic, frenetic way for four days with all activities going according to plan and schedule.

After the last institute group session on Thursday afternoon, the entire group met again. Dr. Bernard, who had served in at least three roles at the institute, chaired the session that focused on its intraprocess. Dr. Bloom presented his rudimentary findings on process and content evaluation. Over-all reaction and fatigue tended to indicate a neutral evaluation of the institute although some positive comments of its usefulness were expressed. Subsequent evaluation has been done individually, most notably by Drs. Bandler and Bloom, who have concerned themselves with the impact of the institute on the organization and structure of the Boston University faculty and on attitudinal change of the participants. In that respect, the participants and their institutions gained. From the content covered by the discussions and the educational process model, others can also benefit.

3. THE INSTITUTE: CONTENT AND PROCESS

H. Keith H. Brodie, M.D.
Archie R. Foley, M.D.

The content of the discussions and the processes within each of the eight institute groups were recorded both by the group discussion leaders and the two recorders in each group. The following material is abstracted from these reports. "The Content" precedes "The Process" so that the reader can relate the group processes and dynamics to the particular issues under discussion.

The reader will note certain similarities among the processes each group went through. The most common is the lack of utilization of their first resource consultant in the first morning session. A phenomenon characteristic of most of the discussion groups in which all the members participated was a crisis, misunderstanding, or similar occurrence that tended to divide the members of the group into factions. Such threats to the group's functioning were consciously resolved, and their resolution seemed to indicate that it was safe to speak one's feelings and opinions honestly without fear of reprisal. Each group seemed to develop its own approach toward discussion and information; the approaches varied in object of focus—studying their consultant, a case study, themselves, or a particular program or issue—but not so much in group efforts to seek specifics rather than to deal in abstractions. Specific information tended to avoid polarization, and generalizations tended to produce polarization. This can also be said of familiarity versus unknown elements among the Boston University and Columbia University participants and programs. An almost universal comment concerned the amount of insight each person gained about his own work, especially with regard to community relations and the work of his colleagues.

The abstracts include primarily those comments and approaches that were unique to each group. Group III is presented first in somewhat more detail to give more of the flavor of a group session.

Group III

Content

Minimal standards?
Resources required?
    Basic survival needs to be met first.
Total responsibility approach to service?
    Consensus: community psychiatry has a responsibility to meet social needs.
    Adherence to model of preventive psychiatry is too narrow.
    Preventive psychiatry is still an unproven hypothesis.
Psychiatric isolation versus reality?
    Treating individual patient needs to bring in reality of his life, his community.
Social action versus individual treatment?
Professional goals?
    Leadership and role diffusion necessary for community psychiatry to meet goals.
    Legislative mandate and support needed.
    Professional responsibility is to articulate and document needs for legislation.
Research?
    Needs separation from administration so that it will not be subservient.
Evaluation? Effectiveness of elements versus effectiveness of total program?
    Any one or all may be effective without the reverse being true.
Mental health roles interchangeable?
    Yes, but responsibilities are not.
    Responsibility versus power—explosive issue.
Research in/on a community?
    Victimizing, often little benefit to community, likewise explosive.
Distinction between research and evaluation?
    All programs need evaluation and feedback; not all need research.
Is the issue involvement, or communication?
Is the Community Mental Health Center outmoded in

favor of the comprehensive service center?
>Not in the sense of providing mental health services but perhaps so in other regards.

Use of nonmental health professionals and nonprofessionals?
>Dissent.

Training?
>Assist other professionals versus training others for psychotherapy—no consensus.
>Train others to improve their work in their own field with mental health input.
>Train mental health facilitators with specific missions.
>Train community psychiatric professionals to work in community and in clinical settings.

Process

Group never broken into factions.

Affective and volatile discussions.

Split avoided over misunderstanding by return to concrete from extremist abstraction.

Confrontation and resolution produced strong group cohesion with high tolerance.

Method of discussion: resolve general, then practical, then training issues.

Separated specific practices in community psychiatry from each other, evaluated each differently without carrying over negative points to other topics.

Interdisciplinary rivalries appeared primarily as identification and show of party loyalty.

Group III

Content

The recurrent issues were: What are the minimal standards of care and services that our society must provide? What resources and personnel are required to provide even these minimal services? These were consistently approached the same throughout, namely, (1) use of professional expertise in various situations, how to stay within the framework of professional goals, both in and outside the community mental health center; (2) the role of the mental health professional and the mental health institution in social action; (3) the mental health institution in its community; (4) the community's perception of the role of the mental health institution (avoidance of grandiosity by mental health professionals); and (5) quality of care: amount required, criteria for, and evaluation of.

Group members felt that psychiatric services could not

be provided in a helpful way until certain basic survival needs of the target populations were met. One approach to delivery of services was that of responsibility; that is, an individual or an agency assumes responsibility for the total care of an individual, rather than approaching him only through a specific problem that is defined by the agency, which clearly neither solves the problem of the patient who is unable or unwilling to make the request for health care nor resolves the question of identification of needs. This led to a discussion of primary, secondary, and tertiary prevention. The assumption of responsibility for primary prevention was felt to depend on the un-proved assumption that adequate social and welfare services can realistically prevent mental illness. Why, it was asked, was it necessary to rationalize social and welfare services in terms of preventive psychiatry? What is there about our society that requires the rationalization of such moral and social choices as psychiatric treatment? What prevents their being discussed in terms of humane care? Regardless of one's orientation and feelings about psychiatry, as defined in the narrow sense of a medical sub-specialty, crises exist in our society and psychiatry has a responsibility to meet the needs of our society—this was the consensus. Whether or not the most effective rationale is that offered by the model of preventive psychiatry was a point of disagreement because danger was seen to exist if the attempt were made to meet these needs strictly in terms of preventive psychiatry and preventive psychiatry turned out to be ineffective. This would produce a backlash.

The discussion evolved toward delivery of services. The consensus was that dealing only with the clinically ill individual who presents himself for treatment to now-existing facilities serves to isolate the psychiatrist from the realities of the new needs of the community. Many participants posed the question of how to avoid returning to academic study in order to escape situations in which the psychiatrist feels professionally hopeless. An active, continuing involvement with those in need and a sharing in active decisions with community members was presented as one solution. That social action in lieu of individual treatment by time-tested conventional methods could, if instituted, correct the ills of society elicited the comment that the distinction between social action or mass approaches and the traditional individually oriented approach must be preserved. That led to a discussion of the role of the community mental health specialist who presumably should function throughout the entire range of services—from individual treatment to interagency work to broadly based political action as needed. What training is appropriate for such an individual? How realistic would the solution be if it called for totally new types of professionals with new training? The answer in discussion was that demands require not only leadership ability but also role diffusion in that the professional must be able to undertake whatever activity is necessary to achieve his professional goals. It was decided that the professional goals are, in fact, unattainable without the support of the legislative process that has the mandate to implement the necessary activity to meet the needs and wishes of the community. It is the responsibility of the professional to articulate and document these needs.

Research was another prime topic in this group. The first issue raised concerned the need to separate research from the administrative arm of a psychiatric facility. If, for example, the two are tied too closely together, most of the time spent in research can be used to generate evidence in support of administrative decisions, thus ignoring research results that conflict with established administrative services. Discussion of the difficulties of evaluating total programs revealed the belief that a total program may be effective even though analysis of each component may prove it to be ineffective. This again led to a consideration of roles and role diffusion.

The tasks that can be shared among all mental health professions and those that remain unique to each mental health professional were questioned. These distinctions were deemed basic to the team concept and to checking the threat of role diffusion to the point of disintegration. It was noted that while many roles can be interchanged, many responsibilities cannot be. The question of responsibility must be decided in terms of protecting the patient's interests and providing optimal care rather than in terms of interpersonal power struggles. This judgment resulted in a discussion of the extent to which the issue of medical responsibility is confused with the issue of locus and focus of power—a potentially explosive area that parallels the problems inherent in the research evaluation of the impact of a specific program on a specific community, especially when such research is performed in some communities that see themselves as the victims of years of research without any demonstrable benefits to the community.

A definite distinction between research and evaluation was made: not all programs need research, but every good program should have some form of evaluation. It was noted that room exists for practical action based on common knowledge without the need for formal research, but continuing evaluation was considered to be essential.

What kind of involvement does the community want in its mental health center? What type of community involvement is useful to the center and its functions as perceived by professionals? How much of what is desired comes under the rubric of facilitation of communication between all individuals involved, and how much of the communication gap is necessary to bridge the gap between the nonindigenous professional and the community as well as among the individuals and the subgroups within the community itself? Is the community mental health

center concept already outmoded? Doesn't the community need instead a comprehensive medical, social, welfare, rehabilitation, and service center? One argument
against such comprehensive services is that the political
reality of their leadership would probably fall to
specialists such as internists or pediatricians who might
not be responsive to the mental health needs of the community as perceived by mental health professionals.

One resource consultant noted that training, such as
he provided to policemen, was very clearly designed to
assist the already established professional, for example,
the police officer, to serve more effectively. This was contrasted with other projects in which participants proposed
that nonmental health professionals, such as teachers
and nurses, and indigenous persons be trained to do some
form of psychotherapy. A lively discussion resulted concerning the use of indigenous nonprofessionals and, the
consensus was that they should be trained not as psycho-
therapists but as mental health facilitators with the clearly
defined mission of assisting clients to obtain available
services rather than of providing new or substitute services.

The group felt strongly that community psychiatry
is not and ought not to be a unique subspecialty of psychiatry and that it should aim toward training psychiatrists and other mental health professionals to work in
the community as well as in the more traditional clinical
settings toward which the traditional training has been
oriented.

Process

An interesting division developed within the group during discussions of role diffusion in which the assignment of power and the mental health professionals' un-
questioning assumption of responsibility as something
uniquely theirs were considered. This issue was difficult
for the group to discuss. In the midst of the discussion, an
increase in the affective level of the participants and perhaps some sign of the division of the group into opposing
camps became evident. This issue was not articulated
and in no sense was the group actually broken, but the
volatility of the issue was an important threat to the
integrity of the group. This occurred the first morning.

During the afternoon discussion, a misunderstanding
developed over the comments of the resource consultant.
Many of the members had very serious reservations about
the concepts of innovation under discussion, and the misunderstanding created a situation in which the discussants
approached the issue more and more abstractly, retreat-
ing from the material and from each other by intellectual
abstractions. Some members of the group noted this and
called it to the attention of the discussion leader, who

reiterated the purpose of the group. This permitted it to avoid increasing the degree of misunderstanding and to return to more concrete material that maintained the unity of the group and the ability of its members to communicate effectively. It was the first time that high-level tension had arisen in the group and gave them something tangible to consider about the group dynamics. The threat of disintegration of group discussion into general, uncontroversial, intellectual generalizations and polarization occurred only because of a genuine misunderstanding. The group's awareness of this threat averted the consequences and proved beneficial in the long run. In short, the group worked well from the start and suffered only the one major split, one that was perhaps essential to permit real cohesion by emphasizing that the priority was really to get a job done rather than to intellectualize and draw a blueprint, even though that was recognized as an appropriate activity.

The method, level, and genuineness of concern for resolving issues under discussion changed greatly throughout the institute. The major change was the degree to which issues seemed to be raised to avoid involvement in action in community psychiatry or to remove obstacles to involvement with community psychiatry. This latter factor became a dominant determinant both quantitatively (for example, numbers of group members) and qualitatively (for example, within individuals); not only did the group want to work out its problems, but its members had extraordinary ability and intellectual competence to do so. They used the person who was the major questioner of the values of community psychiatry in theory and practice to sharpen their own smaller differences, and they were able to elicit responses from the discussion leader and resource consultants that were emotionally and intellectually relevant and crucial. The group rejected firmly and excluded from inclusion in community psychiatry practices that were clearly incompatible with their own standards for responsible professional behavior, and they were able to do this without automatically carrying over such negative reactions to other, equally unfamiliar approaches. That is, this group was able to differentiate community psychiatry from practices of programs presented to them as examples of community psychiatry or community mental health practices and to evaluate them differentially. The group was appropriately concerned first with general issues; then, having resolved these issues sufficiently to permit a positive interest in actual practice, it dealt with them and with training issues.

The interdisciplinary rivalries came up last, as one would expect, but not with much depth of feeling. Such feelings were expressed more as a show of party loyalty. It seemed evident that who was doing it would not likely be the determinant of whether the job got done, if reasonable regard for feelings and prerogatives was exercised in the distribution of opportunities and authority.

Group I

Content

Community rejection of services?
    Political motivation.
    Alienation of underprivileged.
Can community psychiatry have impact?
Social change?
Wielding influence?
    Community psychiatry, a type of ecological reference.
Academic policy?
    Private practice to augment income.
    Ineffective split role; also, split among residents.
Hospital in private practice model?
    Same split role as for practitioners.
The service-social system interface?
    Learn to negotiate.
The underprivileged?
    Social-educational training.
    Psychotherapy, a red herring.
    Set priorities.
Limitations on consultation?
    Limits of institutional structure.
    Preventing institutionalization of new program.
    Professional independence to be maintained.

Process

From general to specific.
Quickly developed group sense.
Universal participation by third day.
Excellent attendance.
Members expressed their feelings.

Group I

Content

Orienting the delivery of mental health services to the needs of the community led to a discussion of community rejection of professional services and the fact that rejection is often politically motivated rather than community-user-based. Some participants pointed out that "politics" may be too ready a rationalization. The alienation and rage of the underprivileged community can be very real, and a mental health worker may have to back off, at least temporarily. The question arose as to whether community psychiatry could have impact because of the fragmentation, isolation, alienation, and lack of communication within the many institutions in the community. Practices in community psychiatry, it was noted, have to be seen not as revolutionary forces for or against social change but rather as forces basically committed to patching up an inadequate system. Discussion focused on how a mental health professional could bypass teachers and others in community institutions who are or may become reactionary so that he could contact people directly. The opinion was expressed that community psychiatry could influence community agents, but there was no consensus on how the mental health worker could articulate his activities to persons holding political or economic power. After the first day, however, the group did reach the consensus that, whatever community psychiatry may be, it implies a type of ecological reference.

Another major issue concerned traditional practice. Because of the policy at Boston University and similar institutions, members of the psychiatric faculty must rely on private practice to augment their income. This drains energy and has a long-range deleterious effect on commitment to and involvement in community psychiatry as a method of practice different from traditional private practice. The situation was described as putting a rather ominous pall on the masochism of the faculty—their persisting in roles that are somewhat ineffectual because of fragmentation and that have a built-in half-life—inasmuch as they wear people out at a rate that neither the person nor society can afford. In the discussion general approval was given to what was identified as the Chicago model of a salaried full-time psychiatric faculty. A further problem seemed to stem from this conflict. The present situation at Boston University and elsewhere tends to attract psychiatric residents who are primarily interested in private practice careers, thus further perpetuating the conflict between community psychiatry and traditional practice.

A cleavage was felt to exist between community needs and the increasingly protective involvement of the hospital in the private practice model. This leads in many ways to a splitting of individual roles rather than to a corrective reorientation of the hospital program. The hospital faces the same problem as the practitioner, and the resolution at present is a dilution or blurring of roles in which hospital or community needs are simultaneously served by the same people, thereby decreasing the effectiveness and satisfaction of all concerned. These statements, though made about Boston University's University Hospital, were considered applicable to all university and general hospitals.

The need for the community psychiatrist to learn to negotiate at the interface between social systems and sub-systems focused on practical issues such as negotiating with community agents and caretakers to help people get programs that would aid them in coping with urgent social problems. Community psychiatry for the under-privileged, viewed as having the highest priority, was defined in part as social-educational training for com-petence among the ghetto young; psychotherapy itself was noted as being a red herring. At one session this was discussed at length, and members of the group eventually decided that it was necessary to establish priorities be-tween direct and indirect preventive services and that the basic problem was dealing with the failure of the underprivileged to cope socially, educationally, and vocationally.

The discussion regarding the resource consultant's work with police brought out two points. In developing a new program, the consultant must first accept the legitimate, inevitable limitation of the institutional structure in which he works. Second, once the program is operational, the consultant must prevent its institutionalization in ways that will put it back into line with traditional, restric-tive attitudes of the institution. A consultant must main-tain his professional independence so that he and his ideas are not misued.

Process

The group seemed to move over the course of the meet-ings from general and theoretical considerations to more specific and practical considerations. This was greatly facilitated by a fortuitous assignment of resource con-sultants since the group first had consultants who were relatively gentle-mannered and theoretically or method-ologically oriented and then consultants who were relative-ly more charismatic, practical, and program-oriented. By the third day, participation in the group discussions in-cluded the entire group. The last day was largely devoted to gathering information, and the resource consultants were challenged only intermittently with questions from the participants. The nearly perfect attendance record of the seven members of the group was impressive. They expressed a wide range of feelings and activities, and rather rapidly a sense of group emerged, which, in retro-spect, was most consistently witnessed by the reception they gave the resource consultants—an invitation from the group as a whole for each consultant to become a member. The group members were ready to engage each resource person as a peer in query and comment and sought out the point of view each brought to the meeting. One by one, the consultants were activated by this appealing expression of the group, although some arrived fatigued by earlier efforts, especially in afternoon sessions. The group response soon revitalized the consultants, and the afternoon sessions tended to run overtime till the discussion leader adjourned the group.

Group II

Content

Mental health facility relationship to community?
Who has control? How much?
The Boston University community mental health center?
    Responsive involvement with community.
    Mental health staff enjoy their work with community.
    Mutually positive relationship.
Harlem Hospital?
    Supports Boston University staff experience with community.
Members discussed their own personal experiences.

Process

First day: resource consultants not used.
Problem in creating a sense of being a group:
    Members not previously acquainted, new to Boston University.
    Resentment toward community psychiatry among many.
    Polarized seating, table used as a barrier.
After first day, members more confused than before.
Second day: group seating, members vocal and attentive.
Last day: group participation, "a natural leader" consultant.
Group response?
    Each was already doing community psychiatry!
    Insight into their own work.
    Major benefit: meeting their colleagues.

Group II

Content

How well a mental health facility relates to the community was stated in terms of how much control the community has over the functions of the facility. The discussion focused primarily on the Boston University Medical Center's involvement with its community mental health project. To date, the mental health workers had been quite responsive to the demands and shifts in mood of the community, and this positive relationship had caused the workers to thoroughly enjoy their work with the local community. This topic was further supported in discussions of the relationship between Harlem Hospital and its community.

Process

The resource consultants were not used at all during the first day. The recorder noted that there was a great problem in creating a group and attributed this to the fact that all members in the group were young, therefore new to Boston University, and therefore had not known each other even remotely before attending the institute. Participants were described as being more confused after the first morning session than before. On the first afternoon, all participants sat at one end of the table, facing the group discussion leader and consultant at the other end. A shift occurred the second day. The group was more vocal in the morning and began to listen attentively in the afternoon to a lecture-type presentation on activities with the police. The response of the group was extremely positive. On this second day, all persons arranged themselves equally around the table; they did not exhibit the sense of separation noted on the first day. A real group interaction did not take place, however, until the last day when all members of the group participated in the discussions. This, in part, was attributed to the consultant, who was described as a "natural group leader." In the last few minutes of the final session, the group members expressed a broadened awareness of the problems in the community and respect for the problems being faced by each person in his daily professional tasks of attempting to teach and to provide mental health services.

Early in the institute many factors indicated a resentment to community psychiatry; later, however, it became apparent that each and everyone present was already doing community psychiatry and that each was extremely interested in and dedicated to his work. This insight caused each person to gain considerable respect for the activities of the others in the department who were also working in community programs. This insight about their own work and that of others was considered to be the major benefit of the institute.

Group IV

Content

Does community psychiatry deserve a title for itself?
> No working definition.
> No discrete body of knowledge.
> From a private to a public health role.
> New focus and concern for groups.
> New participant-observer techniques.
> Consensus: agreement to disagree.

Community needs?
> Economics, education, and health.
> Deprived areas: economics top priority.

Does psychiatry have a role in solving economic problems?
> Mental health planning for preventive services.
> At least as adviser to other programs.
> Providing treatment to those suffering from economic problems.

Community psychiatry a subspecialty?
> No, not for answers to specific problems.
> Yes, for the development of techniques and conjoint approaches.

Process

Polarized group.
Late arrival and early departure of opposition members.
No closure on issues.
Source of conflicts?
> Professional versus social responsibility.
> Promises versus resources.

After the last session, when "the meeting was over"?
> Animated and searching conversations among members and consultants.

Group IV

Content

The question of whether trends and techniques of community psychiatry that do not seem very different from current practices need the particular title of community psychiatry received a response that the essential difference is related to passivity on the part of the psychiatrist. Before 1963, people had to seek out the psychiatrist; the federal legislation that year gave the psychiatrist a more active role. Psychiatry, as a profession, could not restrict its practice to those bringing themselves for help but would have to accept the challenge to be concerned with those who could not recognize their need for help nor seek it. One point of view expressed in the group was that community psychiatry may not be a new specialty or a new set of techniques but that, as a field, it is definable by its new focus and new concerns. One participant suggested that community psychiatry may be doing the very thing it has criticized conventional techniques for doing in the past: making evaluations of needs of communities and promising to deliver with insufficient means to recruit, develop resources, or provide service. The efforts to define community psychiatry produced no one working definition and pointed to no discrete body of knowledge subsumed under the title of community psychiatry. Discussants noted, however, that it is evolving a general technique of being both participant and observer in environments in which mental illness develops. This is relevant to prevention because of the crises in people's lives that can be either intensified or modified by various environmental forces. By addressing these forces on a consultative or collaborative basis, community psychiatry moves out of the private sector and into the public sector, with the roles assigned by the public. As such, community psychiatry responds to public demand to play a public health role rather than a private health role. The public health role is expressed by the professional's interest in people who are not in formal treatment or clinical services.

The needs of the community were broken down into economics, education, and health. Economic problems were agreed upon as the prime community need in deprived areas. The question of whether a psychiatrist must try to meet economic needs to alleviate deplorable economic situations was discussed, and the need for an answer to it was accepted by some as having a high priority in mental health planning for preventive services. Accordingly, the psychiatrist definitely seems to have an advisory function as well as a responsibility toward treatment programs relevant to economic pressures. According to one example, if a program requires mothers to leave their children at home so that the mothers can gain income, psychiatry can certainly indicate that this is a bad practice in terms of child welfare.

In response to statements that community psychiatry tends to abolish the dyad as the unit of treatment and considers the community to be the patient, discussants pointed out that professionals can consider a variety of new and modified means to affect the behavior of more than one individual without compromising such conventional treatment techniques as individual psychotherapy. As such, community psychiatry is not so much a subspecialty with answers as it is a subspecialty that explores other techniques and conjoint approaches. The psychiatrist's contribution was deemed to be his understanding of developmental issues and concerns that can help to change the multitude of institutional arrangements that have a profound psychological impact on the individual.

Process

A type of challenge seemed present at the end of the first meeting. Group members commented that they felt extreme disappointment. The first session started forty minutes behind schedule because late arrivals kept interrupting an introductory dialogue between the discussion leader and the resource consultant. This was unfortunate, for it extended the length of the dialogue and strengthened the image of the Columbia faculty members plus affiliated special "outsiders" as teachers with the Boston University faculty relegated to a substratum as students. The impression of the recorder was that the discussion was characterized by relatively frank and friendly dissent between two subgroups that were definitely in conflict over the issues of professional responsibility versus social responsibility and of overpromising and overstating the case for community psychiatry without the manpower resources to back up the promises. The discussion leader commented, "It seemed to me that the opposition simply lay back and waited for openings of things that could be misinterpreted so that they could redirect the session to belabor more extreme viewpoints." He was troubled throughout by ongoing commitments of "the opposition" that caused its members to arrive late and depart early, which meant that the group could not work through issues that could be clarified only toward the end of each session. At the concluding session, however, almost all participants remained around the table and continued to discuss the issues that had been raised and to involve the resource consultant in an animated conversation. In comparisons among the resource consultants and discussions with the discussion leaders, this group was apparently the most polarized in its opinions toward community psychiatry.

Group V

Content

Introductory case presentation, a disappointment.
Comparative analysis: Columbia University versus Boston University.

Levels of involvement of community psychiatry and community?
> Individual case.
> Consultation programs.
> The community as a whole.

Columbia model for dealing with community?
> Form representative professional and community groups, negotiate.

Dealing with vocal, nonrepresentative spokesmen?
> Use uniform arrangement in catchment area to select representatives.

Advocacy of client needs?
> Social worker apparently better than psychiatrist, perhaps owing to training.
> Help the people assert themselves without jeopardizing their interests.

Consistent themes: black-white conflict; social action versus professional role.

Statement of issues to be resolved.

First morning: reticent, doubtful, silent.

First afternoon: two members dropped out; others became vocal, relaxed.

Group hard to jell.

Use of consultants increased in each session.

Research-oriented members: more active, receptive.

Analytically oriented members: hostility turned to curiosity.

Major benefit: opportunity for Boston University staff members to sit and talk with each other.

Group V

Content

The introductory case presentation was the first topic. Group members expressed disappointment in it, and one person said, "The communication problems and cultural components in the family were not discussed clearly." This led to an analysis of the differences between approaches used by Columbia University and Boston University in establishing relationships with community groups. One participant outlined three levels of involvement between community psychiatry and a community: around the individual case, around consultation, and around policy, sensitivity, and organization of the community as a whole. He felt that collaboration began at Boston University at the policy level whereas at Columbia University it started at the case level. All agreed the paths of the two medical centers were different. How does one communicate and plan with the community, particularly when dealing with a vocal group claiming to represent the community that, in fact, represents only a small portion? The Columbia consultant presented the model required of them by the Community Mental Health Board: to form a group of professionals in the area and then to form a second group consisting of local citizens elected by some uniform arrangement throughout the area. Another consultant noted the problems of identifying community faction leaders, of identifying their shifts in position, and of assuming a neutral position while at the same time getting involved meaningfully with the community. This shifted the discussion to analysis of the professional role versus the role as a citizen that a mental health worker must assume as an advocate of client needs. Social workers were seen as playing the role of advocate more often than psychiatrists and psychologists—a result due in part to their training as advocates of need.

In a lively discussion of ways in which community psychiatry can influence ghetto areas sufficiently to change child developmental patterns and parent relationships, there again emerged the recurrent theme of citizen versus professional. Should community psychiatry play an advocate's role, and does this include fighting with the Establishment; or are there ways to fill such a role other than taking the actively resistant role assumed by the community? The consultant who focused on services to the poverty area responded that the professional role of the mental health worker is to advocate mental health and to help people come to grips with their feelings and assert themselves without putting either the person or the mental health worker on the line, in the negative, sacrificial sense.

The discussion leader noted that in all sessions the consistent theme was the black-white conflict and the struggle for delimiting social action versus the professional role of the psychiatrist and the mental health professional. One session produced a clear statement of the major issues: "(1) quality versus quantity; (2) identity crisis in the professional role; (3) either/or thinking—the individual versus the community in treatment programs; (4) the dangers of diluting the intensity of treatment by approaches in community psychiatry; (5) the problem of delivery of services and how coverage can be made more equitable; (6) the problems of political involvement, the power struggle, the status struggle, and the context of emotionally vested interest; and (7) the problems of the definition of differences in the definition of one problem by the community and the mental health professions."

Process

In the first session, the group was reticent with members speaking only of doubts or maintaining long silences.

They were not willing to express their feelings. Many were doing individual treatment in their practices and did not know why they were participating in the institute. They challenged the case presentation. In the first afternoon session, two members were absent; those present were more verbal and relaxed. After the morning session, it was generally agreed that the institute was particularly useful in enabling the faculty of Boston University to sit and talk together, an opportunity they would never have ordinarily. At the close of the afternoon session, most persons felt a real need to continue the discussions and expressed disappointment that on the second day the workshop sessions would be shorter.

Participation in this group was very active and was characterized by earnestness and hard work. Even though its members were not jelled enough as a group to make fruitful use of the resource consultants, on subsequent days the participants were able to utilize their expertise. Most consultants quickly became part of the group and participated as individual members. Only one gave a lecture.

Of the various members of the group, the most active and open to new ideas were those most involved with research. On the other hand, participants who were most analytically oriented seemed at the beginning rather hostile (expressed mostly by silence); toward the end, they became less hostile and more active, and seemed better able to perceive the validity of more flexible ways of dealing with emotionally and socially disturbed individuals.

Group VI

Content

How to select nonprofessional workers?
>   Eventual criteria: ambition and energy.

Quality of care?
>   Bad for rich and poor alike, only different types of bad.

Medical versus educational and other models?
>   The patients and community want to give their own diagnoses.
>   Educational model gives the person a feeling of effectiveness.
>   Educational model most applicable to community work.

The chronic patient?

Cultural values versus treatment?
>   Provide community option to select programs affecting values.
>   Psychotherapeutic model of growth, dependency, regression, what is progress?

Columbia versus Boston University?
>Columbia University started by using existing hospitals for community services.
>Boston University started with University Hospital, thus selected patients.
>Each needs to move toward the types of programs within the other.

Training programs need solid base: Boston University base is psychotherapy.
Little interaction at first among members or with consultants.
Members worked toward establishing themselves as a group; succeeded in doing so by first afternoon.
Focused first on specifics to become acquainted.
Used their own experiences for content and to build group process.
Familiarity produced appreciation of the character of the Boston University medical community.

Group VI

Content

In the discussion of the use of nonprofessionals and volunteers in providing mental health services, much concern was voiced over the process of selection. In the long run, however, such qualities as ambition and energy were accepted as prime factors. This first session ended on the quality of care given to the poor, and also to the middle and upper socioeconomic classes. The group members felt that care of equal quality was given in the several categories, because the rich often get just as bad treatment as the poor even if it is somewhat less dehumanizing.

Is community psychology or social work training relevant to the education of psychiatric residents? This led to an afternoon discussion of models. The effectiveness of the medical school model versus other models was related to designing community mental health services. In considering the possible contributions from the educational model, the group noted that in developing consultation and similar programs, the traditional medical model is not being followed because, in many instances, the patient and/or the community gives its own diagnosis and demands certain types of treatment. The educational model was thus considered to be more applicable in situations in which people want to have a say in how psychiatry is going to be practiced in regard to themselves. Letting people have this feeling of effectiveness that they have not experienced before can be a crucial element in community psychiatry, and it can only evolve responsibly from an educational model.

Halfway houses, the extent to which the community should participate in their initial formulation and planning, and the responses one might get from the community developed into a discussion of the chronic patient. Participants became increasingly aware that in examining the issue of getting a patient "better," psychiatrists impose their own value system on society. One participant suggested that a different approach might be to offer the community an opportunity to select or reject programs and their inherent values. Whether community psychiatry has an intolerance of dependency and a concomitant constant pressure for growth of the patient was questioned in this connection because it poses a specific ethic. The participants kept returning to this discussion of the psychotherapeutic model of growth. Is not the professional's fear of dependency on the part of his patient an overreaction, and does not the clinician have a tendency to overtreat and in some instances neither to value nor recognize regression as a positive sign?

The discussion leader noted that one of the fruitful interchanges concerned the focus at Columbia University, which utilizes existing hospital facilities for community services, and the focus at Boston University, which is oriented to its established service arrangements with an emphasis on consultation. Discussion revealed that the Boston group had no experience in treating lower-class patients. Such patients were not admitted to the University Hospital service, and the flexibility of approach at Columbia in treatment resources and hospital use was not available in Boston. Thus Columbia started at one end of the spectrum and Boston University started at the other. Each was considered to need to move toward the other in the range of programs offered. Much of the discussion focused on the experience with these two approaches, the populations involved, the problems in resident education and training, and the relationships among the university mental health center, the medical school, and state and local governments.

The Boston participants were concerned about the high value their training program places on individual psychotherapy and psychoanalytic orientation. The introduction into training programs of a variety of approaches, if not built upon a solid base, would be confusing. This concern extended even to the use of family therapy. The consensus was the need for careful thought about training—to provide a solid experience in individual dynamic psychotherapy as a base to good training.

Process

Little group interaction occurred the first morning, but the group became very cohesive in the afternoon. The recorder noted, "There was a warmth and spontaneity and comfort in contributing to the group. We focused on specific things and got to know each other better." As the members appeared to be working toward the establishment of a group in the early sessions, the resource consultants were not as effectively utilized as they were later. As the sessions continued, they became impressed by the seriousness of purpose of the participants, their involvement in the community and their consultative efforts, and the concentration of talented people drawn to and kept in the Boston area by its attractions. Discussions brought out the feeling among Boston University participants that the Boston medical community appeared to be more cohesive than similar communities in the New York universities.

Group VII

Content

Crisis intervention versus innovation?
> Need new methods for new problems, and need to seek and recognize both.
> Freud for innovation.
> Innovation a threat to procedures and a rationalization.

Black versus white?
> Whites presume to understand.
> Need legislation for employment and for guaranteed annual income.
> Repeal "man-in-the-house" legislation.
> Negro professional alienated from his community.
> Vital to earn confidence of community.
> Understanding group dynamics is transferable; environmental factors are not, are crucial.
> Black power: right or wrong, work with it positively.

Evaluation?
> Yes, but what?
> Almost impossible to evaluate a changing, viable program.

Irrational opposition to community psychiatry?
> Perhaps due to accusatory, evangelical attitudes in community psychiatry toward others.

Process

First day: initial irritation gave way to responsible query.
One member set tone of group.

Group method: focus on one specific, develop from this.
Questioning technique exhausted resource consultants.
Third day: rebellion over "monomaniacal focus" on urban
nonwhite poor.

Group VII

Content

The resource consultant's presentation of his work in
training policemen in family crisis intervention emphasized
the need to be innovative in coping with situations as they
arise, the need to note that changing situations will continue to arise that will require new methods of coping
with them, and the need to always look for new methods.
This produced resistance in some participants who felt
that such an approach to innovation was too great a threat
to established procedures. This caused one member to
quote Freud as saying, "There must always be a search
for new ways of identifying problems, social problems,
and creating ways of coping with them." Another participant commented, however, that even though the number
of people in need of help far exceeds the personnel available to provide help, the need should not be used "as justi-
fication for using nontraditional methods, such as behavior therapy" which everyone seemed to agree was a
dehumanizing way of coping with clinical problems in
treating patients.
Differences of opinion also existed regarding the
Negro's position vis-a-vis white society and the ability of
white mental health workers to understand the Negro. This
was talked about to some extent in terms of how much
whites can understand and how much they presume to
understand, when, in fact, they do not. The consultant,
when asked what legislation she would recommend to
relieve the situation, mentioned legislation to enable the
Negro male to obtain employment. She also stressed the
need for a guaranteed annual income as well as the importance of doing away with the welfare legislation that
forces Negro males to "get the hell out of the home."
Discussion the next morning, again on racial issues,
concerned Negro professionals who are obviously middle-
class and alienated from the Negro groups they wish to
serve. This brought out how vital it is for a person to earn
the confidence of the community in order to provide that
community with service, regardless of a person's relationship to it. Racial issues continued to be discussed in the
following afternoon session. Two themes emerged: the
similarities and differences in white versus black poverty populations; and the question as to whether the black

power demand is or is not healthy. Some felt it false economy to talk about white versus black poverty populations, or even lower socioeconomic versus middle-class groups, since understanding the dynamics of one group, they maintained, was transferable to understanding the dynamics of other groups. Opinion was divided on this with the main difference being that although the dynamics might be the same, the environmental factors are very different and are really the critical issues. Some wanted to talk about community mental health in a context larger than for just the poor socioeconomic groups, but racial issues remained dominant. In the discussion on work with schools, black power was the issue. To this the consultant responded, "They want only black professionals, and right or wrong, I, as a school consultant, have no choice but to accept that and work with it and hope that the outcome will be basically a good one."

In one of the final sessions, a presentation of an evaluation of a day center program for chronic schizophrenics provoked the comment that once one is ready to evaluate a given program, innovation has already taken place and that, because a program is constantly changing and viable, it is almost impossible to get an evaluation.

Some participants expressed a sense of fatigue over what they thought was a chronic accusatory posture on the part of professionals in community psychiatry toward colleagues not thus committed; that there was something oppressively evangelical, humorless, and self-righteous about community psychiatry that generates an unnecessary sense of guilt and that, in the long run, is responsible for irrational oppositional attitudes.

Process

The first day a few individuals showed irritation and harassment, but this soon gave way to a highly mature and responsible attitude toward the serious objectives of the institute. One member set the tone for an attitude of serious inquiry and dialogue, and this became the prevailing spirit of the workshop for the rest of the week.

The idea emerged in this group that a person should focus on a specific, urgent community problem and develop a program in response to it and that this would develop a cooperative community attitude that would permit other aspects of the community mental health program to evolve systematically from the initial effort. The group members used this technique in their discussions. This might account for the reputation of the group among the consultants for enthusiasm for questions and a questioning technique that exhausted the consultants.

Around the third day, a full-scale rebellion erupted against what was sensed as a "monomaniacal preoccupation with the problem of the nonwhite urban poor." This, too, seems to tie in with the group-developed approach of how to attack a problem and a program: latch on to something specific and build from that point.

A condition revealed with great clarity was the sense of loneliness and isolation among the members of the Boston University staff. For many of the younger Boston University participants, the institute provided the first opportunity to meet their own associates at close range. What they heard and saw appeared to make them feel proud and assured that the Boston University faculty was of unusually high caliber.

Group VIII

Content

Broad concepts and residency training?
> Existing subdivisions of services and changes therein affect residency training.
> Knowledge to be gained in community psychiatry is equal to that found in individual work.
> That poor people can only be dealt with en masse is false.
> Psychodynamic formulations applicable to all persons; treatment varies.
> Residents need to see wide range and variety of illness.

Learning from community mental health center case presentation?
> Evolution from treating individual to treating groups made evident and legitimate.

The "Need for Action" movement in our culture?
> Evaluation needed for motivation and rationalization of community psychiatry.

Research versus the research model?
> Conflict exists between research and clinical work.
> Offering service to one group and not to another as a control group termed inhumane.

Background of each consultant used as study for evolution of career, program, and issues.

Process

Slow start, growing activity, and positive approaches.
Effective use of the specificity of case studies.
Group members studied their consultants.
Resolving a difference of opinion finally produced group interaction.
Positive use of minority viewpoint to focus discussion.

Meetings ended with "pervasive sense of involvement."

Group VIII

Content

The first hour was spent in stating very broad concepts about what community psychiatry means and what it does. This led to a discussion of training programs, the effect on residency training of existing subdivisions of services, and how changes in such services (especially with regard to the community) would affect residency training. Dr. Lawrence S. Kubie's article "Pitfalls of Community Psychiatry" was referred to, and all agreed that the knowledge to be gained in community psychiatry can be as extensive and intensive as that obtained in individual work. The first resource consultant, approaching the issues from a research perspective, mentioned the false concept that poor people can be dealt with only in masses for whatever real or theoretical reasons; but he noted that, the poor being people, the psychodynamic formulations were as applicable to them as to others, regardless of socioeconomic status. He further stressed the need for residents to see a wide range and variety of mental illness in their training.

The next resource consultant's description of his work in a community mental health center in Brooklyn catalyzed the discussion and led it through the evolution in psychiatry from the treating of individuals to the treating of larger groups. One participant felt it was important to evaluate this movement in terms of scientific curiosity and the need for action so characteristic of our culture. It was also necessary to do this, he said, because this evolution was motivated partially by guilt in confronting the realities of our society. In his view, these factors in combination create a type of social pressure and need for service that could only be met by treating people with the same number of therapists, thus requiring the creation of new therapeutic techniques.

Another participant asked where research fit into the community mental health movement and how what was being done could be studied. One of the research-oriented consultants discussed aspects of social research and the distribution of research projects, such as offering services to only half the group of people so that the other half could be used as a control group. Participants winced at this approach for its lack of humanitarian values even though it is fundamental to basic research. Content of the discussion was focused on the consultants.

This group tended to approach the consultants as case studies in themselves.

Process

The first morning went extremely slowly, and the resource consultant was not brought into the discussion very much. In the afternoon there was more activity; the group became more positive and started its discussion by asking the resource consultant to state his background and go on from there. This proved to be an effective way of getting the discussion going. The group discussion became more sharply focused as the many personal experiences of the participants were related to their needs and interests. The report on training and activities with the police developed a particular "go" that finally resulted in an interchange of comments and ideas. The recorder termed this "an exchange rather than a statement of opinion." After a difference of opinion indicated that the discussion had become open and admitted all participants to a debate of the issues, the discussion leader was quoted as saying, "Today we became a group." The difference arose in a discussion of the educational model versus the medical model as applied to community psychiatry. The minority viewpoint expressed in the group indicated that there was not the full acceptance of ideas that had previously seemed evident.

At the end of the last session, the group expressed surprise that the discussion had in fact become quite open. One participant questioned whether other groups had undergone a similar process and were similarly patting themselves on the back. At the end of the meeting, a considerably free and open spirit prevailed. It was marked by a notably pervasive sense of involvement that had not previously existed to the same degree.

———————————————

4. REFLECTIONS OF THE FACULTY

The following statements are impressions written by members of the faculty of the institute immediately after it was held. The Planning Committee had requested these impromptu comments solely to get a feel of the responses of the persons who had served as faculty members and to obtain clues for evaluating the results of the institute. Most of the faculty had prepared their statements while they were still in the mental frame and fatigue of the session they were writing about. When the comments were gathered as a collective response to the institute, their value became evident. They were complete statements about the process and content of the institute and about the impact of the intense dialogue on the faculty and the participants.

When it was decided to publish the statements in approximately their original form, each person was asked to review and edit his original comment and to make any changes he deemed necessary. The faculty response was unanimously favorable. One faculty member said, "I agree. Even after all this time, my statement stands up pretty well. In fact, I enjoyed reading it. As far as I am concerned, it can go as is." Another said, "It is rather refreshing to read what one had written a year earlier. I find my comments can stand as they are, and I am rather pleased with their briskness." Other comments were "This statement seems essentially okay. I do not dare start changing anything" and the inevitable "OK. When will it appear?"

The statements that follow, therefore, appear in almost the form in which they were submitted and exactly as intended: impressions and reflections of the institute faculty.

A. R. F.

C. Knight Aldrich, M.D.   Discussion Leader,
Professor of Psychiatry,
University of Chicago
Medical School

The institute was an interesting attempt to educate a total faculty in community psychiatry and to overcome the tendency toward polarization that is currently so prevalent. The workshop approach, importing a faculty from outside of the area, was exciting; whether it accomplished its purpose or accentuated the polarization remains to be seen. I left feeling pessimistic.

It seemed to me that the troubles of the institute, if indeed in the long run they turn out to have been troubles, stemmed from the complexity of the agenda, much of which was hidden. I thought that too much needed to be worked out within the Boston University Division of Psychiatry before community psychiatry content could be looked at objectively. Once involved in content, it was difficult, at least for me, to focus adequately on the controversial issues that rapidly became manifest in one way or another. Some of these issues are represented by the following statements:

(1) One part of a profession, or a department, is trying to superimpose its philosophy of psychiatry on the rest of the profession or department.

(2) As far as the clinician is concerned, community psychiatry is a return to a superficial method that long ago was justifiably discarded.

(3) The nonclinical components of community psychiatry are not and should not be the business of psychiatrists.

(4) Community psychiatry interferes with traditional freedoms of the physician.

(5) Community psychiatry opens a medical field to nonphysicians in a way that depreciates the contributions of psychiatrists to psychiatry.

(6) A faculty from one university is not ipso facto qualified to act as teachers to the faculty of another university.

(7) Members of a university faculty are past the stage
when they should be required to attend teaching
exercises.

A competent discussion leader probably should be able to
bring out and to some extent resolve issues of this kind,
or at least come to some kind of temporary compromise
or cessation of hostilities that would permit the constructive use of resource personnel. Some discussion
leaders may be able to accomplish this purpose; the
superimposition of a predetermined adversary position
on the discussion leader, however, makes the job
difficult, and time demands on participants that make
frequent lateness unavoidable cause the job to be even
more difficult.

The institute indeed may have been successful; my
immediate impression, however, was that it would have
been much more successful if the issues listed above had
been more thoroughly thrashed out within the Boston
division in advance.

Resumé of the Group: This group certainly was not
dull. I am not sure whether it accomplished very much,
however, except to air differences within the Boston
division. Although I had previous access to the question
four members of my group had asked about community
psychiatry in the earlier circularization, I anticipated
that these questions would be brought up within the
context of substantive material rather than a priori.
Instead, however, quotations out of context, distortions
of what people said or were alleged to have said about
community psychiatry, and various other kinds of
evidence were used by one or two members of the group
to present a strongly polarized position.

The vehemence of this attack took me by surprise
when the major antagonists arrived quite late in the first
session. The session had started out with the usual atmosphere of a workshop within which individuals seek to
use resource people to provide a base from which to
develop and defend their positions through discussion of
specific issues. While we waited for the group to

assemble, a Columbia faculty member and I began an introductory dialogue that I thought would be very brief, but that turned out to be much longer than expected in view of the lateness of assembly of the group. This dialogue was unfortunate, for it tended to strengthen the image of Columbia faculty plus affiliated outsiders as "teachers" and the Boston University faculty as "students." (Incidentally, I am not sure that this hierarchical assignment of roles can be avoided, particularly when a whole visiting faculty is imported from the same institution.)

In retrospect, it is clear either that resource persons should not have been present for the first session and perhaps for the first two sessions for this particular group, or that I should not have attempted to use them to provide a springboard for discussion. My absence from the pre-institute planning meeting may have contributed to the problem since I did not learn the details of the earlier negotiations with Boston University about required faculty participation in the service area, concomitant changes in divisional teaching, or the planning of this workshop.

The second half of the first day went along similar lines, with the arrival of the proponents of community psychiatry close to the designated starting time and the entrance of the opponents a half an hour or so later. The thrust toward forced polarization was quite apparent in this session and in the latter part of the Tuesday morning session, and the issue of community psychiatry's presumed sacrifice of quality in the interest of quantity was repetitively and vigorously emphasized. It seemed to me that I was caught in the middle of a struggle for the loyalty of the residents and, perhaps, junior staff, and at times I felt that I was being assigned the role of substitute for Dr. Bandler. Without being familiar with the total picture, I found this role somewhat difficult to play and attempted to opt out in various ways.

On Tuesday morning one of two resource persons involved the group in a rather interesting and productive discussion on research and evaluation until the coffee break. Unfortunately, he had to leave at that time, and his doing so left a vacuum the other consultant did not have a chance to fill before the opponents entered the fray. They focused on another scapegoat and proceeded to belabor him with much of the same frontal attack that had been directed toward me the day before. It seemed to me that the anger was particularly intense against renegades: those who had been identified with the psychoanalytic group but who had deserted to the community. I eventually intervened to diffuse some of the anger, and the battle lines were joined. Finally, the consultant complained that he had not had a chance to speak his piece, but the group was too torn to pay much attention to him. This third group meeting, I think, was the low point of the workshop.

Before the afternoon session, the next consultant and I plotted to try to redirect the group activity to something a bit more constructive. I think these maneuvers were somewhat forced, and perhaps both he and I worked a little too hard to manipulate the situation. The consultant, a resource person on community child psychiatry, had decided to identify himself at first with the opposition and then move back toward the community psychiatry postion. I fear, however, he was more successful in the first maneuver. It seemed to me that the opposition simply lay back and waited for openings-words or phrases that could be misinterpreted-to pounce on and use to redirect the focus of the session to belabor the more extreme viewpoints. I was troubled throughout that the ongoing outside commitments of the opposition were such that they could not delay their departures to work through issues that often emerged toward the end of the session. I regretted although I recognized that economic considerations made it necessary to hold the institute in the local area.

On Wednesday morning the consultant launched into his exciting story on police activities before the opposition had gathered its force. By the time they arrived, the story was building up to such an intriguing climax that the familiar lines of total opposition did not appear until the last few minutes when the consultant's concept of training—combining community and psychoanalytic material from the beginning of formal training rather than adding community material at (or after) the end—was challenged. This issue was not really engaged, however, but instead was held over until the afternoon when, perhaps fortunately, the consultant was late, permitting a rather sharp in-group exchange of complaints about the lack of preparation for the seminar, the lack of congruity between my ideas about the agenda and the group's ideas, and my concern about what seemed to have been a relatively unfruitful use of everybody's time. This cleared the atmosphere somewhat, although the group clearly showed signs of fatigue during the consultant's detailed presentation of many of the concepts of training.

Some resolution had occurred, however, because the high point of the seminar was Thursday morning, a low-keyed but informative and moving presentation on approaches to racial and poverty issues, especially with regard to children. The group responded with a considered and objective discussion of many of the issues; there was an atmosphere or real concern for the subject matter and interest in learning about it and in moving toward resolution of much of the conflict that had been holding up the group. The consultant dealt firmly and tolerantly with the familiar questions about the psychiatrist's competence to engage in community activities and about the relevance to psychiatry of many of the efforts at social change. I concluded that the dissenting members of the group had finally worked through their anger at being placed in a defensive situation and had decided to use the workshop constructively.

Probably because of the change in scheduling, the major dissenters were absent from the last group meeting. At one or two points in the workshop, the nonmedical members of the group had complained that too much was being made of community psychiatry per se and not enough of community mental health, with its implied greater emphasis on the problems and opportunities it presents to nonmedical personnel. In the last session, these individuals had an opportunity to focus particularly on the social work component of community mental health.

All in all, perhaps something was accomplished by the group in four days, although probably not as much as in the less combative groups.

I have some question about the introductory session on Sunday. The taped interview seemed too obviously a search for a testimonial. I would have preferred to have seen a film or tape on a subject such as consultation that is more characteristic of and unique to community psychiatry. I am not sure that any clinical presentation, live or otherwise, could have avoided the intensification, in my group, of the feeling that community psychiatry's approach to patients is inevitably superficial and therefore a backward step in the development of psychiatry. With reference to the rest of the Sunday program, I would have preferred a keynote talk that was more specific and less general. If Dr. Bard had told us about his work with the police, I think that the same feelings about community psychiatry in our group would have emerged, but in a more potentially constructive pattern.

Elizabeth B. Davis, M.D., Discussion Leader,
                              Director, Department of
                              Psychiatry,
                              Harlem Hospital Center,
                              New York City

The group reacted to the resource consultants in different ways as illustrated by notes recorded from two sessions. During one small-group session the consultant gave a brilliant and enthralling presentation of the roots, development, and outcome of the police consultation project he was then directing. He provided in his description many explicit theoretical concepts of community psychology (or community clinical psychology) that relate closely to conceptions of preventive community psychiatry and clear examples of the application of these concepts in the modification of institutional practice in the interest of mental health, community relations, administration, training, consultative practice, and evaluation. The group listened intently, asking few but important questions, obviously gaining much from the presentation and stimulating the transition to the afternoon's discussion of training in particular and the overall meaning of community and social psychiatry.

In a small-group session later the same day, the resource person responded actively and permissively to the group's need to get at its concerns regarding training and relationships between training and practice, between academic and private psychiatric institutions and public institutions, between various mental health disciplines and their practitioners. It was a brisk interchange and dialogue, and the short session ended on a high note of Boston University staff going forward to work out its own ways in community psychiatry. There were general and, I felt, sincere expressions of appreciation of the effort made by the workshop leaders and resource people throughout the week and the statement that it had produced a useful and usable product.

Over-all Impressions: The workshop to which I was assigned as discussion leader was a vigorous but extraordinarily collaborative group, well-balanced as to representation by discipline, gender, age, and experience.

It worked well *as a group* from the start, suffering only one breakdown, perhaps essential to permit real cohesion, and offering an opportunity for emphasizing that the priority really must be getting the job done, not drawing the blueprint, although that function must be performed.

The major issues remained the same throughout, namely:

(1) Use of professional expertise in various situations. How to stay within the framework of professional goals both in and outside the community mental health center.

(2) The role of the mental health professional and the mental health institution in social action.

(3) The mental health institution in its community

(4) The community's perception of the role of the mental health institution-avoidance of grandiosity by mental health professionals

But the method, level, and genuineness of concern for resolving the issues changed greatly throughout the week. The major change was in the degree to which raising these issues seemed to be for the purpose of avoiding involvement in the action of community psychiatry rather than for the purpose of removing obstacles to involvement in community psychiatry. The farther along we went, the more the latter factor seemed determining, both quantitatively, that is, in numbers of group members, and qualitatively, that is, within individuals.

A great deal of information was presented and received, and judging from the deepening and focusing of discussion as the workshop progressed, a remarkable amount was integrated. This is not surprising since this group not only wanted to work out its problems but was an extraordinarily gifted and intellectually competent group of individuals.

They used any person who was the major questioner of the values implicit in the theory and practice of community psychiatry to sharpen their own smaller differences, and they were able to elicit responses from the discussion leader and resource people that were emotionally as well as intellectually relevant and critical (in the sense of being important).

They were able to reject firmly and exclude from community psychiatry practices presented by one resource person that were clearly incompatible with their own standards for responsible professional behavior; they did so without automatically carrying over such negative reactions to other equally unfamiliar approaches. That is, this group was able to differentiate community psychiatry from specific practices and programs presented as examples of community psychiatry or community mental health practices and to evaluate differentially. The group was appropriately concerned first with general issues; then, having resolved them sufficiently to permit a positive interest in actual practice, it dealt next with these issues and lastly with training issues. The interdisciplinary rivalries came up last as one would expect, but not with much depth of feeling, more as a show of party loyalty. One had the feeling that who was doing it would not likely be the determinant of whether the job got done, as long as there was reasonable regard for feelings and prerogatives exercised in the distribution of opportunities and authority.

A final note: the writer very much enjoyed getting to know the members of her group and was rewarded by the experience, which is a good thing, because it was very taxing both of energy and skills.

Sheldon Gaylin, M.D., Discussion Leader,
Assistant Clinical Professor of
Psychiatry,
Columbia University

I must reiterate that I, like apparently everyone else, was more impressed by the process and the resultant change in attitude than by the importance of the communication of specific information, either direct or indirect. I was dealing with individuals who were obviously younger members of the department not involved in policy-making decisions or, for that matter, in any major adminis-trative decisions related to the development of the department. There appeared early on a great many indications of resentment to community psychiatry. As we talked, it became obvious that everyone was doing community psychiatry, that all were extremely inter-ested in and dedicated to their work, and that they gained considerable respect for the activities of the other members of the department who were also working in community programs. To me, this was the major benefit of the four-day session.

As an aside, I must say that I was extremely grateful that I was assigned the role of a group leader, able to sit with one group and develop a relationship there, and not have the immense burden placed upon the various travel-ing experts. These people quite noticeably wilted as the session went on, but again I must say that this wilting did not show up in the actual sessions themselves but only in the breaks such as lunch and in the evening meetings.

Final comment is that it was quite clear that the groups themselves had arranged for a closure. This might have been earlier or later in the suggested program, but closure actually occurred in the morning of the last day. Anything other than a social hour after that should have been held, and I think this was amply demonstrated by the reactions at the last meeting in the afternoon.

Natalie Goldart, M.S.W., Discussion Leader,
Assistant Professor of
Administrative Medicine
(Psychiatric Social Work),
Columbia University

The most important reaction to the Boston University experience for me was that it took me fully two and one-half days to leave it after I returned to New York. It wasn't until the end of the third day after I had come back that I could relate to the New York scene.

The meaning of this to me must be that the level of involvement at Boston University was at such an intensity that very little else penetrated. That further means for me that the depth to which we pursued our interest in the material we were covering was profound, meaningful, and related to our mutual interests and therefore had to be useful to all concerned. Since this happens too rarely in either my personal or professional life, I conclude that in the total Boston University experience, the logistics—which had both good and bad within them—are almost irrelevant to the total result, which is that if human beings are placed together for any length of time, the common experience of finding ways to relate and communicate will finally prevail despite the many differences that exist within us as to purpose and goals. I'm really all for that.

Florence Liben, M.D., Discussion Leader,
Associate in Psychiatry,
Columbia University

My over-all reaction is that it was an exhausting, stimulating, exciting educational experience. Each day it seemed to me that we (my group and I) had run the material and ourselves dry. But the next day, after a rather brief warm-up period, we found ourselves reaching new depths and wider horizons.

I was struck in the post-sessions by the similarity in all the groups of topics brought up for discussion and by the fact that the group process seemed to follow similar lines in all of the groups. It appeared to me that very early, each group formed its own idiosyncratic characteristics which seemed to reflect in a variety of ways some of the characteristics and personality of the group leaders. In my group, if I say it with any degree of objectivity, the participation was very active and characterized by earnestness and hard work.

The resource people varied in their methods of participation. On the first day the group had not jelled enough to make fruitful use of the resource people, but on subsequent days we were better able to utilize their expertise. Most resource people quickly became part of the group and took part as integral members. Only one gave a "lecture," but in his case it was relevant to the needs of the group, none of whom were especially familiar with psychiatric epidemiology.

Of the various members of the group, the most active and open to new ideas were those most involved with research, such as the psychologists and the child psychiatrist. One of the psychiatrists was highly committed to community psychiatry. On the other hand, the participants who were most analytically oriented seemed at the beginning rather hostile (expressed mostly by silence), but toward the latter sessions they became less hostile and more active and more able, I thought, to perceive the validity of more flexible ways of dealing with the emotionally (and socially) disturbed. The nurse and social workers were the least active participants (one was a recorder); and although they agreed with the principles and orientation of community psychiatry, their work was essentially in the small sixteen-bed traditional University Hospital unit, so that in their work they felt stifled and unable to use skills that they felt they had.

A consistent theme in all the sessions was the black-white conflict and the struggle for delimiting social action versus the professional role of the psychiatrist and the mental health professional. In one of the sessions the dichotomies were clearly stated:

(1) Quality versus quantity
(2) Identity crisis and the professional role
(3) Either/or thinking: the individual versus the community in treatment programs
(4) The dangers of dilution of the intensity of treatment by community psychiatry approaches
(5) The problem of delivery of services: how can coverage be made more equitable
(6) The problems of political involvement, the power struggle, the status struggle in the context of emotionally vested interests
(7) The problems of differences in definition of the problem by the community and the mental health professionals

One of the most fruitful sessions was the one in which the resource person gave a number of examples from her own experience that were particularly striking and eye-opening to those who were most resistant to community approaches. It revealed an awareness of the impact of social situations on individual psychological functioning.

In summary, I thought that the organization was excellent, that the mechanics were beautifully arranged; the only problem was that the recorders could take part in the discussion only fitfully. The initial meeting with the case presentation created hostility and/or fostered the pre-conference hostility; it may have been a poor kick-off method. However, I believe that because it aroused controversy and discussion, it was not as bad a beginning as some thought. The conflicts and controversy that came up for discussion throughout the sessions were obviously not resolved, but the institute gave an opportunity to focus and to force thinking on issues with time to think, a commodity often lacking in our busy professional lives.

Louis Linn, M.D., Discussion Leader,
                     Associate Clinical Professor of
                     Psychiatry,
                     Columbia University

I arrived on Monday. As a result, my knowledge of the
Sunday evening session is secondhand. The responses I
heard were uniformly unfavorable. I believe our own
Columbia people were even more distressed by the
opening session than the Bostonians. In general, it was
felt that the case presentation was superficial, lacking in
sophistication as far as knowledge of family therapy
technique was concerned, and that the videotape
apparently suffered from a lack of editing. That is, it
could have been shortened and sharpened in order to
make its point more clearly. Most important of all was a
prevailing sentiment that as an opening statement it
failed to define the main themes of the meeting or to
generate interest, let alone enthusiasm.

   In spite of this inauspicious opening, the work sessions
got off to a running start. On the first day a few individuals reacted with irritation and harassment, but this
soon gave way to a highly mature and responsible
attitude concerning the seriousness of the workshop's
objectives. I must express particular appreciation and
admiration for Dr. James Mann, the Boston University
Director of residency training, for his role in our group.
He set the tone for an attitude of serious inquiry and
dialogue that was the prevailing spirit of our workshop
for the rest of the week.

   The proposition that emerged with great clarity was
the sense of loneliness and isolation among the members
of the Boston University staff. Dr. Bandler's recent communication to institute participants, acknowledging the
validity of this finding and announcing plans to improve
this situation, must be counted among the positive consequences of this exercise. For many of the younger
Boston University participants, the institute was a first
opportunity to meet their own senior people close up.
What they heard and saw must have made them feel
proud and reassured. The Boston University professional
staff is of unusually high caliber. If the community

mental health center idea can indeed become operational anywhere, I believe that this staff has the capability of doing it.

In our group the idea emerged that if one could focus on some one specific urgent community problem and develop a program in response to it, this could be expected to result in a cooperative community attitude. Furthermore, other aspects of a community mental health program could be expected to evolve systematically from the basic project if it proved successful. The teenage out-of-wedlock mother was recurrently referred to as a particularly suitable paradigm.

At one point in our proceedings, somewhere around Wednesday afternoon, there erupted a full-scale rebellion against what was sensed as a monomaniacal preoccupation with the problem of the nonwhite urban poor. Many expressed the belief that valuable general principles could be learned by studying other poverty-stricken ethnic groups throughout the United States or even sections of the middle and so-called affluent classes of our society.

Several expressed a sense of fatigue over what they felt was a chronic accusatory posture on the part of the community psychiatric professionals toward colleagues not thus committed. There was something oppressively evangelical, humorless, and self-righteous about community psychiatric professionals, they felt, that generated an unnecessary sense of guilt and that in the long run was responsible for irrational oppositional attitudes.

The idea of taking a seasoned university professional staff and placing its members in the role of students in relation to professional staff from another university, while narcissistically wounding at the outset, impresses me as a powerful postgraduate educational device. If the workshops could have been arranged symmetrically, so that the Columbia group, for example, had its turn in the role of student and the Boston University faculty took the role of leadership in the teaching role, this might have made the whole experience less traumatic for the Boston group and have given the "other side" some of the educational benefits of this splendid experiment.

Alvin M. Mesnikoff, M.D., Discussion Leader,
                                Presenter, Introductory
                                Session,
                                Associate Clinical
                                    Professor of Psychiatry,
                                Columbia University

The Introductory Presentation: I have given considerable thought to the videotape of my interview with the Q
family in the introductory presentation in an effort to
understand, thoroughly and constructively, the critical
reception it received.

In retrospect, anxiety about the institute and how it
would go led to a desire to get it off to a good start with
some sort of dramatic beginning. Shortly before the last
planning session for the institute, the Q family had been
presented at a regular conference at the New York State
Psychiatric Institute in New York City. There were many
elements in the case presentation that reflected our new
clinical program designed to bring high-quality care to
those who had not previously received such care. These
elements were illustrated by the coordination of a variety
of hospital and community resources centered around
the treatment of a low-income, poorly educated, Spanish-
speaking family, the mother being the patient who was
identified as having been hospitalized at the Washington Heights Community Service. That presentation was
effective and typified to us an example of the successful
implementation of our program. It was thought that it
would be an appropriate introduction for the institute.

The interview was not intended to be a spontaneous
interview of a husband and wife, but rather to delineate
the treatment and record the responses of the patient, her
husband, and her family, which we knew to be positive.
The tape was technically unsatisfactory; it was a single
take and unedited. The voice of the interviewer was too
loud while the voices of the patient and her family were
inaudible to most people in the audience.

We wanted to make a point that such patients can be
effectively treated with psychodynamic psychotherapy,
that treatment requires flexibility of movement from the

index patient to the members of the family and community facilities, and that patience and empathy are
needed to develop a trusting relationship. We also wished
to show that rehabilitation with focus on ego capacities
and development of skills is an integral part of treatment. In a training setting such patients require an
understanding and sympathetic resident who appre-
ciates the rewards of such a therapeutic experience as an
important part of his training. This experience must also
be valued by his teachers, who view it as constructive
and important training that goes beyond the usual
psychotherapy with the typical middle-class, educated,
verbal patient. It need hardly be said that the development of a service in terms of teams, continuity of care,
and availability of an armamentarium of treatment
derived from the acceptance of responsibility for a
particular catchment area is good clinical psychiatry.
However, good clinical psychiatry is not generally
available unless services are organized for delivery to a
specific population. Community psychiatry is problem-
oriented, based on meeting the demands and needs of a
particular population today. Much of the problem
involves the delivery of service. It seems to me that the
availability of comprehensive treatment (here in a
training setting) represents the essence of meaningful
community psychiatry. At present such delivery of care
is all too rare.

*The Boston University and Columbia University Entry
to Community Psychiatry:* The Boston University
group emphasized consultation and community
programs as the aspect of community psychiatry which
they valued and in which they had had considerable
experience. This difference in emphasis led to a fruitful
interchange of ideas regarding the changes at Columbia,
which started its community program by changing the
focus of an existing hospital facility, versus the Boston
orientation of using their resources for consultation as
the initial focus. In our discussion it became clear that
the Boston group did not have experience with patients
of the lower class. Such patients are not admitted to the

university service. The flexibility of treatment resources and the use of the hospital were not available in Boston. It may be said that we started at one end of the spectrum of care whereas they started at the other. The way in which a new program is started reflects the interests of the people involved and the available resources. In the range of programs offered, we need to move toward community development while they move toward comprehensive hospital services for the seriously ill. Much of the discussion focused on the experience with these two approaches, the populations involved, problems in resident education and training, and the relationships between the university mental health center, the medical schools, and state and local governments.

The Boston group was particularly concerned with training programs that placed high value on individual psychotherapy and psychoanalytic orientation. They feared that the introduction of a broader range of treatment would not be built on what they considered a solid base. There was a general consensus about the need for phasing-in various aspects of training so that there would be a fundamental experience in individual dynamic psychotherapy.

The consultation aspects of community psychiatry have great appeal in terms of the status of the position, the feeling that much can be done with relatively little time, and the variety of settings in which the consultant can operate. However, I feel that the hard core of our efforts is going to be in the provision of quality care for all patients, using coordinated community facilities in treatment programs. Consultation has its important place, but the critical element will be the quality of clinical services for which psychiatrists accept responsibility and leadership.

The Institute Sessions: Our group emphasized the problems of the inadequacies of care for the middle and upper classes. When the needs of these groups extend beyond psychoanalysis and individual psychotherapy, they too find that the resources of the community are not adequate. A comprehensive care program cannot be thought of only in terms of meeting the needs of the poor since such needs are found in all segments of the community.

In the planning of the sessions, resource people were introduced from the very beginning. In our group we found that they were not effectively used in early sessions since our interest lay in getting to know each other and in the development of a group. However, once the group had formed, our attention was turned more effectively to the contributions of the resource people.

I found the meetings to be stimulating and thought-provoking. The organization, which emphasized small-group discussions over a period of several days, was very useful. The establishment of a group with increasing trust and ease produced meaningful discussions among the participants.

The intensity of the discussions provided an opportunity to share experiences effectively and to go on to consider new approaches to the problems of community psychiatry.

Marvin E. Perkins, M.D., Discussion Leader,
                          Professor of Psychiatry,
                          Mount Sinai School of
                          Medicine,
                          City University of New York

The view set forth here is largely unrelated to the questions of the extent to which attitudes were changed, understanding increased, distortion favorably modified, and new information absorbed. The vantage point of this group leader, however, leads him to conclude that the conditions were favorable for all such developments to have taken place, and in significant degree.

The conference format clearly provided for the small group to be the main exchange: major conference transactions were designed to take place within the small group. The impressions here are almost entirely conditioned by meetings of my own group, very little else having a commensurate influence.

Seven members of the group assembled an impressive, nearly perfect attendance. (Of two others originally assigned, one never came; the other but once.) This level of attendance by the active members was particularly commendable, as the conference was set within home precincts (and hence, in potential conflict with local and varied obligations of the attendees).

Of greater importance was each member's thorough participation in the work of the group. In this, there was affirmation that the group had a task to perform that was even susceptible to some degree of refinement in the opportunity presented.

The several members were active, candid, direct, concerned, thoughtful, and respectful of difference in viewpoints. Professional issues related to planning, social responsibility, interventional approaches, community consent, and citizen participation were discussed. At times the members seemed also to be annoyed, impatient, confused, and weary.

There was, indeed, a wide range of expressed feeling and participation on the part of the engaged members, producing a rather rapid emergence of group cohesion that, in retrospect, was most consistently witnessed by the reception given to resource persons by the group. The group seemed very ready to welcome the resource persons as full participant members. Interested in the viewpoint each brought to the meeting, the members were yet quite ready to engage the resource person as a peer in query and comment. The resource persons, one by one, were activated by this consistent and appealing expression by the group. Although some arrived fatigued by earlier efforts (especially in afternoon sessions), group interest soon revitalized the resource person, so that the discussion leader on more than one occasion had to declare the session closed after the appointed time for ending it.

Had the objective of the meeting been to impress this group leader with the professional excellence and humanistic qualities of the members of the Division of Psychiatry of the Boston University School of Medicine, that purpose was splendidly attained. That was not the intention, of course. If the members were enabled to garner new dimensions in admiration and respect for their fellow department members, the conference may have effectively opened channels for discussion of such matters as more rational strategic and tactical plans, instrument and method design, and new unified operations in community psychiatry.

Morton Bard, Ph.D., Resource Consultant,
Professor of Psychology,
Director of the Psychology
Center,
City College, City University of
New York

It is difficult to organize one's thoughts after an intense and complex human relations experience. First of all, I must emphasize that the institute proved to be more successful than I had expected. I had had serious reservations that attitudinal change could occur in the manner proposed, but it is my impression that I was wrong. More happened than I had believed possible.

As a resource person, I rotated among eight different groups in half as many days. I found this to be an exhausting but exhilarating experience. As the days wore on (and I felt worn), it became apparent that the quality of the discussion was changing. At first lacking focus and revealing an undercurrent of discomfort, questions became sharper, issues better defined, and ideas conceptually better integrated; group members seemed better able to utilize the resources afforded by the visitor. It is difficult to say whether this resulted from the group's feeling increasingly compatible or whether it reflected the increasing knowledge and sophistication resulting from the input of resource consultants and group leaders. The apparent change was probably an outgrowth of both. I suspect also that coincidental intermixing of leaders with specific styles and the personalities of individual group members had an important modifying effect upon outcome.

There certainly was little consistency in the way group leaders related to the resource person. For me, it ranged from being totally ignored by the leader until the last forty minutes of the session to being placed on the podium to deliver a lecture and manage the discussion afterward, with the leader filling the role of group member. Personally, I found the best leader to be one who related the resource person's background to specific issues that needed amplification and that had arisen in earlier discussions. This was usually done by the leader's providing me with a very brief summary and then explaining to the group those aspects of my background that might be helpful in clarifying these issues. The leader then retained a leadership role by helping to further define issues as the discussion progressed, whether by playing devil's advocate or by synthesizing issues.

The response to my participation appeared to be quite favorable. Although the groups focused on a variety of issues, some appeared to dominate almost every discussion.

Implications of Training in Community Psychiatry: These discussions dealt primarily with the role community psychiatry should play in the training alternatives in this connection: (1) that community psychiatry be considered as an area of special knowledge approached as a subspecialty within the more traditional training programs; or (2) that the traditional programs undergo basic changes secondary to a philosophical commitment that results in an infusion of community into the very fabric of the programs. The implications of both approaches were considered with apparent clarification of the issue, particularly with respect to professional role identity.

Considerable attention was devoted to the necessity of *training for innovation.* It appeared logical to most of us that the earliest years of professional training are critical in determining later professional self-concept and professional functioning. If professionals are later expected to function innovatively, early training should include experiences conducive to the assumption of the innovative stance and readiness to change. The methodological problem, of course, is in retaining those traditional skills essential to role identity while still introducing new ones essential to functioning in a constantly changing society.

Extending Impact through Existing Social Institutions: There was considerable interest in this model as it is emerging in The Psychological Center and The City College of New York. This concept has its origins in the recognition that there are any number of groups already in the mental health front lines whose characteristic functions would be enhanced by training and ongoing consultative relationships with mental health professionals. This approach is in contra-distinction to the training of new professional (or sub-professional) personnel in which the new group must of necessity be self-limiting in resolving manpower shortages.

One of the many advantages of the merging model for utilizing existing social institutions as a mental health resource is the avoidance of role-identity conflict. A po-liceman, lawyer, housing administrator, nurse, or teach-er need not surrender his identity while performing vi-able mental health functions. He need not conceive of himself as a mental health professional while neverthe-less rendering such service in the discharge of his usual duties. The danger in creating new professionals is that their identity formation contains the seeds of later organization and conflict with a mental health estab-lishment already replete with a variety of subdisciplines.

Police-Community Relations: Considerable time was devoted to illuminating this highly charged area of com-munity existence. Particular emphasis was given to stereotypical thinking on the part of the community of the police and vice versa. The groups seemed particularly taken by their own stereotypes, which revealed the basic antithesis between the "intellectual" and the "cop."

The sources of tension between policemen and the residents of the inner city were considered. The essential helping function of the police, their instant availability around the clock, and the complexity of their inter-personal services were discussed in some detail. One of the most glaring sources of tension was considered to be the subtle paradox that among the lowest social classes no group is more hated, feared, and envied than the police, and yet they are the group to whom the ghetto resident turns in the time of sickness, injury, and trouble.

Entry of Community Mental Health Workers into Social Systems: Here the emphasis was on how to inititate programs and work with existing social and political entities. There appeared to be considerable interest and uncertainty about the complex dimensions of working with ongoing agencies. A variety of concrete examples helped to clarify but did not pretend to present a formula or a specific "how-to."

These issues were only some of the highlights in my discussions with virtually every group for whom I served as a resource person. It is my impression that whatever success was achieved by my participation was rooted in my ability to anchor concretely many of the abstract principles of community in specific action programs currently in progress. I also had the impression that this very bright and alert group of people had no concrete examples to illustrate the variety of issues talked about in the past. Much of their cynicism appeared to be based upon a growing conviction that community mental health personnel talk a good ballgame but are rarely out where the action is—actually doing what they say they do.

Format of the Institute: I believe the eight groups could have been better served by half the number of resource people. It would have given the groups an opportunity to interact more and also to use the resource people more effectively than they could within the time limitations imposed by the present format. In addition, the resource people would not have been subjected to such exhausting pressure had they had fewer groups to visit.

I needn't comment upon the opening plenary session. I was personally appalled by the demonstration which served to mobilize resistance and to reinforce cynicism regarding the emptiness of community psychiatry's promises. An excellent opening gambit would have been the presentation of a stimulating and provocative community mental health action program that really demonstrated innovation and yet served to highlight the many questions that already existed in the minds of so many of the participants.

In sum, the institute appeared to be an unexpectedly rich and rewarding experience for all participants. The Boston University faculty developed group cohesion over the four-day period and were, certainly during the latter part of the period, searching and focused in their use of the group leaders and resource persons. As for the visiting faculty, I, for one, found the experience equally fruitful and exhausting. I value particularly having had the opportunity to share my thinking with a receptive professional group and being made to think through and articulate many of my own unformulated ideas and assumptions.

Richard L. Blumenthal, Ph.D., Resource Consultant,
Social Psychologist,
Columbia University

From a personal point of view I found the institute a very
stimulating experience, intellectually provocative, and
an opportunity to pull together into a more cohesive form
a variety of ideas about research, evaluation, and other
related issues in community mental health. I was
impressed by the willingness of all members of the
Columbia staff to engage in a series of conversations
without using the clichés or rhetoric that sometimes
accompanies such discussions back home. I was equally
impressed by the concern with which the Boston people
addressed themselves to these issues. As a research
person with avocational interests, as it were, in other
aspects of community mental health, I was particularly
impressed by the ability of the research people on the
Boston faculty to address themselves as psychologists
and professionals to issues in community mental health
no matter what their major lines of research interests
and competences were. For example, the people I knew
on the Boston University research faculty work in areas
such as physiological psychology, developmental
psychology, and psychopharmacology; nevertheless,
their comments were invariably pertinent and relevant
to community mental health issues.

I thought that the group structure and process
developed nicely as the institute wore on. I use the word
"wore" because it became very trying at times. I felt that
the team situation worked well and that the other
resource consultant and I functioned very nicely, comple-
menting each other when needed, during the two days
that we worked together. The group process was such
that by the time he had to leave, the groups were ready to
listen to issues and problems related to research and
evaluation. I found that I had to work much harder from
the second afternoon on.

Several people mentioned the Sunday evening session
as an experience that structured the rest of the institute.
Technically speaking, it had no effect on the content of

the issues I dealt with as a research person. That is to say, it did not lead into issues around evaluation or other topics with which I would be concerned. I must confess, however, that I do not see it as being a seriously compromising start to the institute's proceedings. Those people on the Boston faculty who were strongly unconvinced in the beginning remained unconvinced by the end of the institute. It is my guess that this lack of conviction has less to do with the substantive issues between community psychiatry and psychoanalysis than with the structural changes that are going on within the Division of Psychiatry at Boston.

Camille Jeffers, M.S.W., Resource Consultant,
Professional Assistant,
Southeastern Laboratory,
Atlanta, Georgia

The conference was a stimulating one. If it could be described in one word, I think that would be "ferment"—ferment about role definitions and ferment about services. People dared to open the community's Pandora's box and were alternately drawn and repelled by what they saw. There was a willingness to think, to challenge, and even to change.

Of particular interest to me were the undercurrent of uneasiness about black power confrontations and, at times, a loss of perspective. In a few short years the stereotype of the passive, alienated, apathetic black community has been replaced by the stereotype of the hostile, aggressive, and militant black community. A greater involvement of the black community in our deliberations would have benefited our search for meaning and should certainly be the next order of business.

I liked the general format of the conference with the group meetings and feedback after the afternoon sessions. However, I did think that the groups should have had a chance to meet by themselves in the first session in order to get acquainted and organized. I think it would also have been helpful if there had been a little more structuring of the use of the consultants. I found that the groups that made the most of me were those in which the group leader had worked me into the program. I was least successful when I had to try to make my way into the group.

Ruth G. Newman, Ph.D., Resource Consultant,
Professor, Department of
Human Development,
University of Maryland

It is now midnight and a mere few hours since the institute ended. Rather than following Dr. Foley's suggestion to wait to write my report until I could view the conference with some perspective, I have chosen to take Dr. Bandler's suggestion and to write now while impressions, however distorted, are still fresh in my mind, I will focus on the Thursday sessions.

Thursday Morning: When I arrived in this group at about 9:05 A.M., all but two members were gathered; they came soon thereafter and fitted in immediately. When I arrived, a lively discussion about group process was already going on: how this group had used themselves, how they had been torn between using the various resource people who had been set before them from Monday on and dealing with their own professional concerns and dilemmas and the things that were occurring in the group before them. Although they expressed satisfaction with the previous resource contributors, they were clearly annoyed with themselves for not having settled, or at least put on the table, concerns of great moment to themselves in their inner convictions and their work-lives. One, at least, commented that they might well have used the resource people as a defense against grappling with these problems and as a rationalized diversion from the major task: their own ability to integrate, use, and apply what had been presented into their own experience and point of view. I, as the resource person for that morning, felt not at all uncomfortable. This was partly because of the firm skill and obvious interest of the discussion leader, partly because of my fatigue with the role of carrying a group on my shoulders by narrating and involving them in my professional experiences, and partly because of the clear involvement and sincerity of this group in its struggle to gain the understanding this opportunity gave them before time ran out. I joined in at this point to indicate that in my experience as a school consultant, I had often been used on the surface as an oracle of wisdom and beneath the surface as a means of avoiding difficult or painful issues. I said I was sure that in their work they must have experienced the same phenomenon and that this in fact was a danger in, or at least a part of, the process encountered in being used as an expert consultant. This kind of interaction went on for the full three hours with much participation by everyone—the leader, all participants, and to some extent myself when it appeared appropriate, when I felt I could draw a useful analogy (or moral?), or when I couldn't contain myself. Although I did not chance to "do my thing," I felt that they got the essence of consultation in a large, rigid, bureaucratic organization such as a school and that they covered with feeling many basic, profound issues of power, civil responsibility, boundaries between professional and citizenship responsibility, administrative perils, and keeping one's own professional identity and core beliefs while still recognizing the needs and contributions of others. Very open criticism was expressed by members of the group about areas in which they and in some cases the residents felt they had been bulldozed into actions without their being consulted. The residents had come to Boston University specifically to learn from Dr. Bandler and to benefit from his insightful clinical perspicacity, and were disappointed to get more training in reading blueprints than in the skills they felt they needed. Understanding of Dr. Bandler's genius in administration was expressed enthusiastically but with a wish that better lines of communication could be created, especially regarding spot decisions affecting them. The residents felt this workshop had given them time and thought to find where they had been lacking in administrative understanding and where there had been lacks in dealing with them. The discussion of bringing about change in all sorts of institutions—training schools, nursing schools—was gone into in depth. The discussion leader handled the whole meeting with honesty, openness, and great skill.

Thursday Afternoon: This, I presume, was what had been called the young group, and it did seem young to me compared to the others, especially the morning group. The discussion was pleasant and active, but it was clear to me that termination was just barely below the surface. They asked me direct, pointed, and probing questions about consultation in schools, entry, power structure, possible agents for change; yet their weariness showed through in how willing they were to skip from issue to issue, as if to ward off the possibility of getting into discussions in depth that would have to be terminated, once and for all, by the hands of the afternoon's clock. Before the very end of the group, the discussion leader brought back the history of the group to its members—the way it had organized, the way it had handled his one-day absence,* the issues it had brought up. Nearly each member, if I recall correctly, commented on the group's meaning to him or her in his or her work or in his or her new feeling of being part of a large organization that he or she felt was more familiar, and therefore more to be respected at this time than before these meetings began.

The Whole Conference: My role as resource consultant was a conflict-making one: When should I move in or stay out? How much should I take over? To what extent was I being used by the group to do its job (or sometimes by the leader to do his)? How much detail would be useful? What issues should be emphasized which day in which group? One could (as in any other new consultative job) only use one's own perceptivity as a barometer. I can make no claim to being able to evaluate accurately how good a barometer I was. I can say that I felt most depressed and ineffective in the first group, the first morning. I am still unsure if this was due to the composition of this group, the discussion leader's apprehension beforehand (evidently justified), or the fact that it was the first. I suspect it was due to the first and last factors.

---

* The group leader was called back to New York on an urgent matter and thus was absent from his group for one day.

In Tavistockian terms, it was clearly a fight-flight group though I understand it developed into a work group by the third day. I was most exhilarated by the experience with my third group. I found their use of me challenging and thought-provoking, and it deepened my own insight. With this subjective measure I cannot but feel the same happened with them—I am sure it did because the discussion leader responded to the issues as passionately as I did. I found the low-keyed, quiet pace of the next leader reassuring. It enabled the discussion of major issues by sometimes angry people to be rational and useful and not just the expression of a fight group; in other words, he quietly kept his group on task. I may have given most blood to one group that was indeed a group—so smug about its own little culture that it had made for itself that it reflected it in the group's point of view toward the outside world. But the implication I got, maybe wrongly—behind the words insisting on the recognition of the need for money and services for the large, un-washed poor—was that, after all, the upper-middle and middle class will and should be our leaders, and therefore more time and money should be given to them. It was not just one member of the group that expressed this attitude, but the whole group, with possibly one or two quiet exceptions. For this reason, I labored double and was allowed to do so. I do not remember being more tired at any time at any conference than I was after this group, except perhaps after one that afternoon when, after six hours of telling and responding, I was dizzy and drained. I think that afternoon group got the worst of me, though I worked hard to compensate, because of the morning's experience. I suspect the most interesting group for me personally was the one on Thursday morning because, by the way they used themselves and the way I participated, I had time to experience some of the things they were experiencing and to relate their experience to my own and to conceptualize from both. I learned much in all the groups, but most there.

In any event, I am grateful (though weary) for the opportunity to join the Columbia staff at Boston University. Not the least of my gains was meeting such a remarkably nice group of interesting human beings—and I emphasize the humanness.

At some points during the conference I tried to fantasize how I would plan such a conference another time. I submit my two separate fantasy-conference plans based on the existing model. Obviously a retreat would be best, given the limits of an in-town hotel.

(1) Simple change: I would not have resource people at the first or last meetings. I would leave those for group gathering and group termination.

(2) More complex: Opening meeting, small groups with group leaders, no resource people throughout, scheduled from 9 to 11 each morning and from 2 to 4 each afternoon. At 11:30 A.M. and 4:30 P.M., I would have a presentation to a large group or plenary session by a resource person lasting forty minutes, with twenty minutes for discussion. This would mean lectures would come one-half hour after a coffee break in a large room at 11 to 11:30 and would close at 12:30 for lunch until the 2 o'clock groups. At 4, a coffee break and at 4:30 lecture and discussion until 5:30. At 5:30 to 6 there would be an open bar. Resource people, besides being lecturers, would be assigned on a rotating basis to be participant observers to each group.

Reasons: Group process and the job of members to get at their own work problems would be enhanced. There would be more opportunity, in an in-city setting, for full plenary participation at coffee breaks and cocktail hours, thus stimulating further and different lines and types of communication. Resource people would not dilute the group experience but still would be able to share experiences in a didactic fashion. The stimulation from these lectures could be utilized directly or indirectly later in the small groups.

My only regret is that I did not get to hear any of the other resource people's experiences in detail. Is there no possibility of a bonus reward for us all by having all these people meet for an evening in New York or in our nation's capital? I invite you all there.

Alex Richman, M.D., M.P.H., Resource Consultant,
Associate Professor,
Division of
Epidemiology,
Director, Psychiatric
Epidemiology Training
Program,
Columbia University

I was not originally optimistic as to what substantive material in psychiatric epidemiology could be communicated within the group format and in the time available. At the end, I was impressed with the rapid and fluent way in which it had been possible to discuss the areas of community psychiatry relevant to psychiatric epidemiology.

I felt these sessions were most productive of discussion when a brief overview of my area preceded the discussion. I thought my resources were used least on the first day and most on the second and third days. Before I visited the group on the fourth day, the discussion leader and I had reviewed the group's progress at breakfast. The group discussion was lively, informed, and focused. The afternoon session was spent completing farewells among the group, and my involvement was minimum.

Some of the issues that were discussed included the nature and role of epidemiology, definition of a case, classification of environments, relevance of prevalence and incidence indices to prevention, class differences in care and outcome, and methods of evaluation.

Maurice V. Russell, M.S.W., Ed.D., A.C.S.W., Resource

Resource Consultant,
Director of Social Service,
Harlem Hospital,
Associate Professor of Administrative Medicine,
Columbia University

The encounter between the faculties of Boston University and Columbia University demonstrated the inherent value of interdisciplinary, interinstitutional, and inter-professional exchange predicated on advance planning, mutual concerns, and topic-related focus within a structural and administrative frame. Despite the many variables (conflicting philosophies, varieties of professional experience, the group sequence, and differing organizational settings), the interchange created a learning, sharing climate that was indeed rewarding as well as provocative. The daily summary conferences of the Columbia faculty provided a stimulus as well as a total sharing of experience that I found personally most helpful. The group composition, with the varying leader styles and patterns, placed the resource persons in a chameleon-like role that was particularly fascinating in terms of my own professional growth. It forced a use of myself and available knowledge to be constantly sifted, reflected, and imparted through a variety of mechanisms and forms that followed no specific pattern, although there was a lengthening thread that could be used with increasing competence as I wended my way through the various sessions. There was an interest and readiness for exchange that I had not anticipated from our pre-liminary meetings in New York, in which certain anxieties were raised as to the suitability of one faculty conducting a workshop for another faculty. At no point was I aware of any conflicting rivalries or antagonisms that were not conducive to creative learning.

The haunting question in the field of community mental health must be constantly raised: Is this different from what we have always done, and, if so, what is different and what are the implications for training? Does it

truly lessen clinical knowledge and content? Will community mental health centers provide second-class treatment for the disadvantaged? Should the philosophy and
concepts be geared to providing care of the highest
quality rather than an expedient way to meet the
growing population needs that traditional training
centers are not equipped, staffed, or prepared to meet
through lack of understanding or knowledge of disadvantaged people? We have known for a long time now
that many patients have fallen between the cracks in the
delivery of services. We have carefully eschewed the
concept of mutuality in the clinician-patient relationship, preferring the original medical model of the
authority-dominated dyad in which the unmotivated
antagonistic patient was invariably considered untreat-
able since he did not follow the rules of the clinician's
game.

With the rising influence and involvement of lay
groups in structuring services to meet their needs, the
role of the clinician must be re-examined in the light of
the delivery of service as well as adaptability and
creativity in the application of clinical knowledge to
patient care. This is certainly new, different, and very difficult for the rigidly trained clinician who has never
expected his practice to be questioned. Yet, why not? If
we believe that the treatment relationship depends on a
challenging dynamic process fraught with certain
tensions and hostilities that must eventually surface, it
follows that such mutual interaction has many healthy
aspects and should accelerate rather than impede the
treatment process. We have discovered at Harlem
Hospital that former patients have much to offer new
patients in a variety of task-oriented roles because their
identification with the problems and needs of patients
has already been clearly established. This immediate
engagement of the patient's ego tends to reinforce his
healthy attributes rather than dependent, regressive
trends that have traditionally made for extensively
prolonged treatment experiences with the so-called
average middle-class patient.

In the disadvantaged areas of the city, years of

deprivation and discrimination have given these populations a tradition of sharing mutual problems and helping each other. This has been the strength of the poor, whose crowded living situations have rendered privacy virtually impossible. They have banded together against the rigors of the authoritative binds placed upon them by the various helping agencies, particularly the governmental agents who are committed to abiding by eligibility requirements and placing large segments of the population into dehumanized groupings (that is, housing authority regulations, public welfare standards, and so forth). It is comparable to the collective ego strength of adolescent peer-group phenomena that clinicians must respect if the adolescent is to move eventually into a healthy sense of individual identification. This places an unusual burden on the clinician to identify and understand the culture of the community in which he is working. Without this respectful understanding, he will never be able to reach his patient group and to be perceived as being helpful to it. When this is demonstrated to the satisfaction of the patient, the treatment experience will move quickly because the clinician is then recognized as a helping ally rather than an extension of the authoritative control already familiar to the disadvantaged populations.

From the point of view of social work, I am concerned that graduate education does not equip workers sufficiently to meet the issues and problems of developing community mental health centers. This is particularly unfortunate since the social work tradition was founded on the needs of disadvantaged people in the matrix of their community life. With the divisions of social work methods (casework, group work, and community organization), there is an artificial separation of the clinical from the nonclinical. This gap must be reconciled, since each method has special importance and much validity, but they should be used interchangeably by every social worker geared to a diagnostic appraisal of the patient's life situation. The social worker of the clinic team is in the most unique position to translate the needs to the total staff from both the clinical and community points of view. The clinical services must be tailored according to existing community resources available to patients. The nature, extent, and availability of resources should determine the structure and philosophy of the clinical program since this will affect the preventive as well as the rehabilitative aspects of programs. Some of these services must be built into existing clinical programs; others can and should be provided by the various community facilities that surround and hopefully will be made available to the mental health center.

Much was learned from the institute. Above all, however, it documented most dramatically the many things we still need to learn to become truly competent community-oriented and involved clinicians.

Kendon W. Smith, M.D., Resource Consultant,
                              Associate in Psychiatry,
                              Columbia University

It is, of course, difficult to evaluate the institute while participating in it. The program was a strain for all concerned and particularly, so I believe, for the resource people. This is in part a subjective comment, but it applied in varying degrees to other participants; only one showed relatively little strain. The strain was cumulative and peaked on Wednesday. There was also the hothouse shipboard effect of close contact within our small group over the four-day period. (Many had, of course, remarked that an Arden House setting would have provided far greater opportunity for informal mixing with Boston University faculty and would have reduced some of the strain on the fatigued institute faculty.)

The Sunday evening presentation, in retrospect, seems to have been a liability. There was certainly value in presenting specific clinical material. Were we to do it over again, I am sure we would all agree on reviewing the presentation, shortening it, and focusing more on the Washington Heights Community Service as part of a process of institutional change. There may have been a slight additional value in that the presentation provided an outlet for preliminary we-they antagonism on the part of the Boston University faculty. The remainder of the institute was quite successful. Morning and afternoon meetings in their home town permitted the Boston University staff a useful change of pace during the evenings, yet exposed them to a wide variety of viewpoints. I felt that a majority of the Boston University staff were quite receptive to the variety of information offered. As the institute was organized, exposure to it facilitated a quantity and quality of attitudinal change, so that the considerable input of content could be better utilized.

Regarding possible alternative arrangements, I think it might have been useful to have had a series of informal evening meetings on Monday, Tuesday, and Wednesday, on a Dutch-treat cocktail basis, in each of three settings of the university complex. The obvious possibilities were one evening each at the University Hospital, the City Hospital and the Roxbury Neighborhood Center, with each get-together having the appropriate staff as hosts. The idea occurred to me originally because of my own sense of psychic starvation and the time involved in several institute groups in enabling members to get a sense of the setting in which other members had gotten experience. Additional intrastaff cross-fertilization of ideas would have been furthered by this means. I know I would have been interested in some exposure to these settings, partly because I customarily feel much more in touch with things when I have had some brief perceptual contact with the plants, getting the feel of the place. I mention this also because of the feeling on the part of the Boston University staff as well of not knowing what each of the other participants was involved in. Such a cocktail party could have provided a very useful opportunity for various kinds of informal exchanges.

Two key areas of the evaluation that follow from this are (1) the impact of contact with other viewpoints within the university as distinct from the impact of the resource people, clearly an unanswerable nature-nurture question but worth struggling with descriptively; and (2) the value of the intrastaff contacts for future parallel efforts elsewhere. I won't elaborate on this. It is obviously a central question the planners probably kicked around. I can think of ways in which its effect at Columbia would be salutary. Anyway, as I sense it, this is the most innovative feature and deserves special attention in the evaluation.

Leo Srole, Ph.D., Resource Consultant,
Professor of Psychiatry (Social
Scientist),
Chief, Psychiatric Research,
New York State Psychiatric
Institute, New York City

Let me just offer a few declarative statements.

I was impressed by the over-all high quality of the Boston University people.

I think the composition of the Boston University groups could have been mixed in terms of senior versus junior personnel and those committed to community psychiatry versus those opposed.

I gave more of myself as teacher, broadly defined, in those few days than in the whole of the year, 1967-1968, at the Columbia University College of Physicians and Surgeons. The latter fact goes by the name of under-utilization.

I got to know my Columbia community psychiatry colleagues and associates better during those few days than in all my three years at Columbia, and I was impressed by them. The implication is that we should participate in such interuniversity workshops more often, as hosts as well as guests.

I can't comment on the resource people, except for the two who participated with me in one or more discussion sessions and my opinion of contributions ranging from irrelevant and dull to relevant and interesting.

Three sessions I sat with discussion leaders through the whole session, and in three others through part of a session. One leader was condescending to junior members. This passeth my understanding, and probably the understanding of Dr. Bandler, who was visiting the group with me.

My one general criticism of the leaders, with one notable exception, was their passivity, by which I mean sitting back and permissively letting the discussion flow in a meandering fashion without steering it. By steering I mean offering the group task-goal structure and guidelines to major issues—specifically, when an important issue arose, to intervene before it slipped away barely touched by questions designed to seek elaboration and clarification of its main conceptual components and its practical programmatic implications and to hold off diversionary, premature movements into other issues before the group felt that the task-goals of the first issue had been satisfactorily nailed down. I call attention to the fact that among six leaders I observed, one was an exception in actively challenging the group to clarify the issues and in contributing to the elaboration and clarification process.

If I may speculate about the passivity referred to, the discussion leaders were not adequately prepared either in terms of assuming the active, Socratic probing role or in terms of being "on top" of the issues that they had lived with longer than had the Boston University people.

5. THE AFTERMATH: FACULTY PROCESS FACULTY POWER AND DEMOCRACY

Bernard Bandler, M.D.

The institute was conceived as a process and method for resolving tensions, clarifying issues, and achieving a common base of shared understanding in the Boston University Division of Psychiatry in respect to community psychiatry. The process was that of intensive small-group discussions over time. Each group was carefully chosen with the assistance of Dr. James Mann to represent a multidisciplinary cross-section of the division; an equal selection of senior and junior faculty members and of those most committed to community psychiatry and those most skeptical, of those more verbal and liking to dominate meetings and those more reticent. The method and the process was the introduction of the Columbia University group, so chosen because of its psychoanalytic orientation, the fact that its experience was in the urban community, and our own high regard for its personnel.

The idea for the institute was entirely mine. Although it was mentioned to key members of the faculty and later announced, the decision to submit the application for its support to the National Institute of Mental Health was an individual one and did not result from faculty process. The second application to NIMH was almost a repetition of the first, with the exception of dropping out the substantial budgetary request to hold the institute at Arden House. Dr. Mann reviewed this application, made valuable suggestions in relationship to it, and concurred with it. There was no faculty discussion of the idea of an institute and of the application. The decision to hold the institute and the lack of faculty preparation for it was thus a good example of benevolent leadership in which the community of the Division of Psychiatry did not actively and democratically participate. It represented the style of leadership and an important aspect of the organizational and structural functioning of the division.

Working with the community, particularly through its teaching technique of the process of confrontation over time, one learns slowly and painfully about one's style and assumptions and about the issues of control and power. One learns how much one is part of the establishment, how much plantation attitude there is behind one's benevolence, and how much colonial attitude behind one's goodwill. Medical schools and their departments are not notorious for democratic process and faculty power. I discussed all aspects of the Division of Psychiatry with different persons; those who were most concerned delegated freely, and never moved toward basic change on important new departures without senior faculty consensus (which had not been achieved over four years in respect to community psychiatry, hence the institute). However, there was no basic faculty structure, no mechanism, and no process for faculty participation in decision-making. The issue of faculty participation, of democratic process of leadership, is crucial, I believe, to departments of psychiatry and their chairmen throughout the country with their multiple taxing responsibilities.

DISTURBING ASPECTS OF THE INSTITUTE

Two aspects of the institute in particular both surprised and disturbed me. The first was that so many people in the division did not know each other and, even more importantly, did not know much about the activities of the division. I had anticipated this in respect to the staffs of the Thom and Putnam clinics, which had recently affiliated with us (though in the case of Thom "recent" means six years or so). But that heads of important sections such as medical school education should be uninformed about programs and policies of other important activities such as our inpatient service surprised me very much. My fantasy of the division was a group of people who knew, liked, and respected each other and were knowledgeable about each other's activities. That they liked and respected each other was true. I was mistaken, however, in respect to their knowledge of each other and the wide range of divisional activities.

The second disturbing surprise was the amount and degree of expressed faculty dissatisfaction with my benevolent, paternalistic leadership and the extent of feeling about their lack of participation in the process of decision-making in respect to policies, particularly those that affected their future and their destinies. Rationalization comes easily even for a psychiatrist. It was easy for me to say to myself that there was naturally a good deal of tension and anxiety about the future with my retirement just two years away. There were also deeply uneasy doubts about the reality of the community mental health center. It had been eleven years in the planning, and the construction costs were not yet funded by the legislature. Were the buildings with all their multiple facilities that everyone wanted simply so many promises, mirages with which I had seduced many distinguished people into making serious career commitments? Although most everyone for different reasons wanted the community mental health center, there was still conflict and uncertainty about the implications and commitments of such a center. In addition, with certain key faculty we had in the last five months—that is, virtually to the time of planning the institute—developed the first of our staffing applications, the one on Consultation and Education. Because of the pressure of time and the inexorability of federal funding and budgetary timetables, not every issue could be discussed at sufficient length to reach consensus. As chief investigator I had to preside firmly and limit some discussions with senior faculty. As sophisticated realists they understood the exigencies of the timetable; as human beings and as eminent psychiatrists they were restive. A substantial number of senior faculty and all the remainder of the faculty were uninformed about the application. For these reasons—my approaching retirement, the absence of definitive funding for the community mental health center after so many years of promise and hope, the pressures of developing the Consultation and Education application, and the lack of knowledge by the majority of faculty of what it was all about and what commitments it involved for the future—I could explain to myself the dissatisfaction of the faculty.

We are today in the midst of a revolution. In human development we realize the importance of increasing autonomy, of self-identity, of control of one's self, and of decisions affecting one's destiny. But in the organizations to which we belong and in our various communities, there is no structural matching, no organizational or community reciprocity of our developmental ideal. There is a failure of power of control, of genuine participation in decision-making. It may be that there are no longer any genuine communities and that the democratic ideal and promise are largely in abeyance. So although in the Division of Psychiatry different people have delegated responsibilities such as heads of the Outpatient Department, Inpatient Service, Medical Education, Residency Training, Child Psychiatry, Research, Community Consultation and Education, they were fractionated and did not participate in the major divisional decisions and policies. There was no process or organization or structure for over-all planning and new developments, for the evolution and determination of policy, and for faculty appointments and promotions. There was no way, short of direct communication with me, to give adequate expression to the originality and the creativity of the faculty and to their many burgeoning ideas about all aspects of our programs. Along with respect for me and affectional ties to me, there was an incipient revolution against the paternalistic and authoritative administration of the division.

DEMOCRATIZATION OF THE BOSTON FACULTY

The community workshop process had thus begun the even more important faculty process. Two agenda were at work simultaneously in the institute process: the manifest, overt agenda of community psychiatry and the latent, covert agenda of the democratization of the Division of Psychiatry. At least, so it seemed to me immediately after the institute. Interestingly, immediately following the long-awaited, eagerly desired announcement that the Massachusetts State Legislature had appropriated capital funds for the construction of the mental health center, there was an intensification of critical feelings.

I did two things. I sent the following memorandum to the participants in the institute:

> The institute made it obvious that we have a great need to plan regularly for us to meet together for sharing of information, for thinking, and for continuing our faculty communication both professional and social. I should welcome your suggestions as to how you think we can best do that.
> Three ideas have occurred to me:
> (1) Regular faculty meetings once a month
> (2) A social hour once a month, say, Fridays from four to five
> (3) A yearly faculty dinner-dance
> These are just off the top of my head, and I am sure you have many more creative suggestions.

Since there were not many immediate replies, I sent the memorandum again a month later. The replies totaled thirty-six, including one signed by thirteen members of the division who designated themselves as Junior Faculty:

> In May, the Junior Faculty psychiatrists decided to meet regularly as a group. We did this in response to a shared wish to orient ourselves to the activities of the Division of Psychiatry as a whole, to develop comments and ideas about the future directions of our institution, and to express our feelings about policies and procedures in our

work. We plan to continue these meetings as an important part of our regular professional activities.

The division has grown over the past several years with great rapidity. This growth has resulted in innovative and exciting programs, but it has also created problems that are significant and demanding of consideration as highlighted by the June conference.

Among issues crucial to the development and cohesiveness of the division are:

(1) The articulation of its goals and philosophy
(2) Relationship of the division to the hospital and university
(3) Clarification of the present administrative organization
(4) Intrafaculty communication
(5) Examination and questioning of fundamental assumptions of division policies, especially in the areas of traditional clinical activities, community services, teaching and research, and the interfaces among these areas
(6) Consideration of future developments of the division such as the mental health center

We want to join with you and other faculty groups in making our voice heard in the effort to solve problems facing the division. We see this group as, among other things, a positive response to the questions raised by your memo, and will be glad to make specific recommendations when we are prepared to do so.

FORMATION OF THE POLICY COMMITTEE

The second thing I did was to form a Policy Committee. The initial members were all full professors responsible for significant programs, including the three psychologists who had full professorships. The Policy Committee, which throughout the summer and fall met twice a week for an hour and a half each session, soon added additional members: all full professors and those members of the faculty with major functions such as medical education, community psychiatry, and epidemiological studies without regard to academic rank. The Policy Committee now numbers fifteen. The early meetings were unstructured and without agenda. Since everything on everybody's mind was talked about without interruption, there were full expressions of feelings and ideas. For a time, policy and administration intermingled, and all but the most routine letters written by the chairman were reviewed both as to content and to style. Thus two sessions were taken up in the selection of the five or six members of six different committees collaborating with six different schools of the university in planning for training at the community mental health center. The charge to the committee and my letters of appointment were also discussed, including the question of whether or not the letters should come from the Policy Committee and whether or not the committees should report directly to the Policy Committee. A more relaxed atmosphere gradually settled over the Policy Committee. Since it became enmeshed in increasing administrative concerns however, there was little time left to discuss policy. It was decided in February, 1969 that the chairman should appoint a small Executive Committee to handle administrative meetings whose minutes would be distributed to the Policy Committee. Each committee would meet once weekly. The Policy Committee then began to address itself to the process of restructuring the Division of Psychiatry so that by the time of my retirement it would be functioning as an organic and democratic whole.

But what of the rest of the faculty? The Policy Committee reviewed the thirty-six letters received in response to my memorandum of June 14 and decided that the wisest way to proceed would be to follow the recommendations submitted in Dr. Mann's letter:

> I did not respond to your memo of June 14 because I had no good suggestions to make. The value of our four-day institute to the entire faculty had been demonstrated, I believe, to each member of the faculty. The problems that evolved out of the institute were, to put it somewhat mildly, rather overwhelming. I chose, therefore, to sit on my thoughts. As it turns out, I sat long enough until I had the opportunity to read the suggestions of those who did respond to your request.
>
> The more difficult problem is how we can maintain an atmosphere and environment of *knowing each other well enough to air discontents as well as creative ideas and information about each other's everyday functioning* and how to do this across the various sections and disciplines in a Division of Psychiatry that no longer consists of a small, harmonious single-minded group. Our problem, it

seems to me, is rather pointedly, albeit on a smaller scale, the problem of any present-day community. The sense of powerlessness growing out of increasing diversity and specialization, sheer organizational size and function, accompanied in practically every instance by mounting problems in managing one's own personal and family affairs within a still larger complexity can give rise to a defensive and compensatory grasp for a share of the power. The aim is not to feel so powerless; not to feel so much controlled by others. (Thus, some of our dissidents could say in response to your question as to why they did not speak with you, *"they* said you were too busy." Who is the "they"?) The search for power becomes directed, in part, by distortion and projection which create an over-all atmosphere of suspicion about the other person or the organization. If one attempts to share openly an honest concern, he runs the risk of enhancing suspiciousness about his own position and motives rather than there emerging a genuine, searching give-and-take with the aim of seeking mutual understanding and perhaps even resolution. This was brought to my attention rather forcibly when I dared to suggest at our Grand Rounds panel on research in psychiatry that an underlying problem is the researcher's hidden aim of gaining control over people and that they should subject their motives to scrutiny at least as much as clinicians try to subject their own. I was truly shocked to see how quickly some of our faculty took this as a *personal* assault by me on them.

While I do believe that appropriate organizational structure can do much to smooth lines of operation, make clearer channels of communication and lines of force, it cannot get at the basic problem of each individual faculty member struggling to establish a secure and confident base of operations for himself in which he can at the same time feel trusting of his colleagues and of the over-all total organization. Social hours of any kind are not the answer because they are social. Large faculty meetings can be primarily informative only. Annual workshops are not enough to carry over through the year.

I would propose an experiment. Grand Rounds takes up about forty Wednesday afternoons in each ten-month period. Suppose that for one such ten-month period, we did away with all the varieties of presentations that we have been having or are even planning to have. Instead, suppose we had ten groups of ten people each (perhaps plus one designated leader); each group cutting across all sections of the division; each group meeting for ten Wednesdays and then reorganized into ten differently composed groups for another series of ten meetings. Each group could decide what it wished to do in the three or four series of ten meetings available to it. In other words, a ten-month-long workshop that would provide for the intimate intrafaculty exchange not otherwise possible. Would this make possible genuine carry-over for some indefinite period of time? And would not a year-end dinner-dance then be welcomed? Other arrangements are possible. Such as a scientific meeting (Grand Rounds) to be the fourth or fifth meeting for all groups in each series of ten.

I will stop here because the details are less important at the moment than the idea. I believe that we must seek a solution or solutions that are different from past experience with such matters because while we are dealing with common universal human problems, it so happens that the setting in which these problems are presently happening has little resemblance to past settings; both intradivisionally and within the larger environment in which we are all living now. Perhaps what I am saying simply is that we cannot manage growing alienation by imposing further structure and order however well intentioned since these are experienced as further bureaucratic imposition and tend to increase alienation. We have to bring people together in fact and in act. I make my suggested experiment as a basis for discussion. Evaluation procedures would be essential, of course.

This proposal was presented to the faculty. The faculty, through a show of hands, indicated a vast majority approval, although the Policy Committee later had reservations as to whether this genuinely represented strong approval. The Policy Committee, therefore, decided on the following procedure, which was carried out in my memorandum of November 14 to the faculty and participants in the institute:

The institute last June started a basic innovative process. This process was faculty communication and sharing. It also indicated the way to something more fundamental, namely, policy formulation and decision-making. It indicated the method by which faculty thinking, initiative, imagination, and creativity can be given full play in developing all aspects of our program and organization for the future. Our strength is the excellence of our faculty; our task is to permit it full expression.

At the last faculty meeting there seemed to be sentiment for the proposal to continue the workshop formula by weekly one-and-a-half-hour meetings throughout the year. A show of hands, however, can be very deceptive. Both I and the Policy Committee suspect there is much more a division of opinion, more reservations, and many questions to be answered. More importantly, the faculty did not have an adequate opportunity to participate in the decision or to raise the questions as to what happened to the many fine suggestions written to me since the institute.

We plan the following:

(1) *Workshop:* Wednesday, December 11, from 10 A.M. to 4 P.M.
(2) *Agenda:* To propose procedure and mechanisms for continuing the process of the institute.
The recommendations that result from this workshop will be implemented for at least the remainder of the academic year without further review or change by either the Policy Committee or by me. This workshop is not to be another on community psychiatry. It results from your responses to my memo of June 14, 1968, which resulted in many letters to me. [Memorandum of June 14 quoted.]
All the letters sent to me, including Dr. Mann's recent one, will be made available to all members of the workshop.
(3) *Members of Groups:* We will try as much as possible to preserve the same groups as participated in the institute. There are new members of the faculty, and they will naturally be added. Also, a number of members of the Policy Committee found themselves in the same group and have asked to be reassigned.
(4) *Structure of Groups:* Each group is to select its chairman, secretary, and delegate to the Committee of Delegates. The Committee of Delegates will meet at a later time to review all recommendations of the different groups and to organize the final working plans. Each group can naturally select its chairman as delegate as it chooses. The Policy Committee has requested that its members should not be selected as chairmen or delegates. It will be appreciated if the secretaries will keep adequate minutes and forward a summary to my office.
(5) *Committee of Delegates:* The delegates will meet one week after the workshop on December 18 from twelve to four. If they wish to meet longer, so much the better. Each delegate will have a copy of the minutes of each group. The charge is to organize the recommendations of the groups into final plans.
Membership of groups and plans of meetings will be sent to you in ten days.
A *Plea:* Please make your recommendations as detailed and specific as possible. Any recommendation that entails the expenditure of money should be precise as to how exactly such money should be raised.

During all this time the Junior Faculty continued to meet regularly. They invited various members of the Division of Psychiatry to inform them of their programs and activities. The Policy Committee had now joined me as members of the establishment, and we were confronted by a generation gap! Since the Junior Faculty had inquired of others about the Consultation and Education program, I invited myself to one of their meetings, sending them copies of the application several weeks in advance. Three of its members have in the course of the year become members of the Policy Committee since each was heading a major program. Others had been appointed to significant committees representing their major interests.

DEPARTMENTAL DEVELOPMENT AND HIRING OF STAFF

The major task of the Policy Committee was now the development of departments. We are still in that process: the psychologists presented a proposal for the Department of Psychology in the Division of Psychiatry; the section on Community Psychiatry spent seven months devoting its proposal for a Department of Community Mental Health (which has occupied the last five meetings of the Policy Committee); and the Department of Child Psychiatry is concluding three months spent by all its members toward developing a proposal for its organization and democratization.

Since the Consultation and Education program had been developed in collaboration with the community, the question arose as to the process of hiring staff. It took three meetings before it was agreed that there be two committees of five members each: a Community Screening Committee selected by the community and a Faculty Screening Committee selected by me. The Community Committee would screen all applicants in respect to their sensitivity to the needs, values, and aspirations of the community; the Faculty Committee would screen all applicants in respect to their professional competence. The two committees would meet together to exchange their evaluations on all applicants. Each committee would have an absolute veto. During these discussions the Area Advisory Board of the mental health center also played a very valuable role. The Policy Committee thus acted to share power with the community with full knowledge that if the two committees should reach an impasse, the Consultation and Education program would be paralyzed and nobody would be hired. The two committees, after a period of confrontation, agreed that the administrator and coordinator of the program would be evaluated in terms of competence and not of the professional degree. They selected a remarkable black woman who had not been to college. By unanimous vote she was made a member of the Policy Committee.

The Committee of Delegates of the workshop completed its report on January 28:

> The work of the committee resulted in three distinct recommendations. The language of this report uses the word "recommendation" as defined in Dr. Bandler's memorandum of November 14, 1968 (page 1, item 2, paragraph 2). The word "suggestion" is used to indicate propositions that should receive further consideration before implementation.
>
> *Recommendation No. 1: Communication-Structure of the Division*
> *Introduction*
> The one major internal challenge for the division at the present time, as seen from the point of view of the leadership of the faculty, is to find ways that will allow the faculty members to be most effective in their contribution to the accomplishment of the division's mission, and this includes the development of new goals and programs as well as the attainment of excellence in the more familiar ones.
>
> Seen from the point of view of many members of the division, uneasiness manifests itself as a feeling of a lack of participation in the life of the division. This ranges from relative isolation to fairly strong—yet suppressed—feelings of not being consulted and informed adequately in the processes of making decisions that affect their professional lives and that require their participation.
>
> Seen from the point of view of the development of the division, the challenge is very much the basic one of coping with the extraordinary success and growth of the division, under the peerless leadership of Dr. Bandler. The number of people involved, the range of projects, the diversity of programs, the multiplicity of budget—all are leading the evolution of the division toward greater and greater complexity, especially in the next few years.
>
> The response to this challenge is for the division to develop an orderly and practical structure that will provide mechanism for communication and participation as well as stimulation and cross-fertilization.
>
> The members of the Committee of Delegates felt that to

make specific recommendations for structural changes may be beyond the mandate of the committee. The necessary information about the present structure was not available to any delegate present, and may be available to no member of the division other than the chairman. But, above all, such an enterprise should properly involve the active participation of all the faculty members.

This Committee of Delegates therefore recommends:

(1) that the question of the structure of the division be the object of intensive study of the whole faculty;

(2) that the structure be studied in a series of nine group meetings of one and one half hours each on the following Wednesday afternoons during the time usually devoted to Grand Rounds: February 19, February 26, March 12, March 19, March 26, April 9, April 16, April 23, and April 30;

(3) that the eight groups remain constituted as they were for the December 11, 1968 Faculty Workshop except as follows:

(4) that the residents and research fellows in psychiatry be included in the above groups and that psychology trainees and other trainees be included upon the decision of their principal supervisor;

(5) that the reports of the work of each of the eight groups be forwarded by May 14 to the Policy Committee, as well as to all members of all groups;

(6) that the chairman respond to these reports at a General Faculty Meeting on June 18, 1969;

(7) that the groups meet individually on the following Wednesday, June 25, to prepare and express their reaction to the chairman and the Policy Committee's response;

(8) that each group include in its report or final evaluation a recommendation on the continuation, discontinuation, or future use of the present group format;

(9) that information about the present faculty organization, personnel structure, programs, etc., and, in particular, an organizational chart specifying names and responsibilities be prepared and made available to each group on or before February 19; a general faculty meeting could be used as an effective method of supplementing written information;

(10) that key resource people, e.g., Policy Committee members, heads of programs, disseminate recorded or written statements to all groups in responding to the questions addressed to them by any group so as to be able insofar as possible to remain active participants in their own groups;

(11) that Grand Rounds be suspended until next September.

This committee would suggest that in the event that these groups continue to meet in the future, the question of enlarging their membership to include nonprofessional and other ancillary personnel be studied anew.

This committee declined to recommend whether or not the groups had to meet all nine scheduled times, and whether or not participation in the group should be compulsory.

Recommendation No. 2: Newsletter
Introduction

The Division of Psychiatry has been expanding very rapidly in recent years and will continue this accelerated rate of growth in the near future, both in terms of personnel and in terms of programs.

A communication medium is needed that will allow periodic centralized and coordinated dissemination of information about events, activities, and developments in and of the division, especially to those members who are part time, or whose location is outside the Medical Center complex. A large proportion of the faculty spontaneously expressed the wish for a newsletter as presented in the reports of six of eight groups at the December 11, 1968 Faculty Workshop. Such a newsletter would be the natural vehicle for the dissemination of all faculty-wide announcements.

This Committee of Delegates therefore recommends that the Division of Psychiatry publish a monthly newsletter for its members.

This committee also suggests:

Recommendation No. 3: Social Events

Many members of the faculty have expressed a wish for activities that would bring the members of the faculty together in a relaxed and informal atmosphere.

This Committee of Delegates therefore recommends that a social hour be held once a month in conjunction with Grand Rounds, the Visiting Professor program, or a similar activity that is directed to all the members of the faculty.

This committee also suggests that the tradition of inviting community people to the Annual Christmas Party of the division be continued.

The three recommendations were immediately implemented. I had mentioned one of the recommendations in respect to the social hour in my original memo to the faculty. I had thought of mentioning a newsletter but decided to omit the suggestion. What is important, however, is the process by which ideas and proposals are brought forth, not simply and exclusively the ideas and proposals as such. Academic freedom means freedom of the faculty to direct its destiny as well as freedom to teach and to pursue knowledge. In these days when every group hoists the banner of power above its name—student power, community power, black power—the faculties have been strangely silent; no bugles have sounded for faculty power. There is good reason for this reticence because of the authoritative departmental structure of our medical schools. The chairmen command impressive power: power of appointment and of promotions, power of salary, power of space and job assignments. It takes courage to speak out and to disagree. So the recommendations were not only an assertion of faculty functioning but also a test of my good faith and that of the Policy Committee. After review with the Policy Committee the following memorandum was sent to the faculty, participants in the institute, residents and fellows:

Introduction

The meaning and purpose of these recommendations is to allow the maximum freedom possible to each group in its efforts to approach the problems of the Agenda. Through our collective experience of the December Workshop and more specifically through the experience of the frequent meetings of the Committee of Delegates, we are quite convinced of the effectiveness of task-oriented groups. Each group should have a good opportunity to measure itself against the challenge, and the first four sessions are for this individual work.

On the other hand, it is imperative that the groups be offered the enrichment of the other groups' thinking early enough in the continuing workshop to thoroughly consider all those alternatives that may be raised, and begin the monumental task of identifying major trends in the faculty's thinking.

The Committee of Representatives as outlined in the procedural recommendations is elected exclusively for the purpose of coordinating the work for the groups and summarizing their final recommendations. There has been a desire, expressed at various places, for the Committee of Delegates—the one formed at the December Workshop—to assume responsibilities beyond the mandate specified at that time. That idea is in itself a modification of the structure of the division, and should be considered, examined, and decided on upon its own merits rather than taken up out of the convenience of the moment. (See further under Agenda.)

Procedures

(1) All procedural matters, date of meetings, date of

reports, etc., except those indicated here, are as outlined in the report of January 28, 1969.

(2) Each group will elect its own officers. One of these
will act as representative of the group. The representative does not have to be chosen before the
fourth group meeting; he does not necessarily have
to be someone else other than the chairman. All
faculty members are equally eligible for all offices.

(3) The groups should decide on their own recording,
keeping in mind the necessity of informing the other
groups by April 2 of the progress of its discussion—
or lack of it. If a group wishes to keep a running
record of its deliberation, it should keep it focused on
the issues raised rather than on the identity of the
debaters, to insure the greatest possible freedom of
expression.

(4) The representatives from each group will meet after
the fourth session; that is, on April 2 from 2 P.M. to
4:45 P.M. at 889 Harrison Avenue to exchange information about each group's discussions and coordinate the subsequent progress.

(5) The Committee of Representatives' final task will be
to meet again, after the last group session (April 30),
to prepare a comprehensive summary of the reports;
this summary to be presented no later than June 1 to
Dr. Bandler, and for distribution to all the faculty
members.

Agenda

(1) The major charge to the faculty members working in
these groups is to examine the structure of the division and make recommendations to respond to the
needs created by its extremely rapid growth (see previous report). To this end we would recommend that
each group, using its own members as resource persons—at least at the start—proceed through the
method of "case studies" to examine in the concrete
how programs were initiated, decided upon, and
carried out. At least two or three instances should be
studied. The relevant pathways taken for information and the crucial points of decision should be
identified; the repetition of patterns should be recognized as the real elements of the effective structure
of the division. Every effort should then be made to
generalize the issues to the broadest level for their
applications to the whole division. The purpose of
this workshop is not to solve any particular problem
but to develop better ways for the division to deal
with all its current responsibilities, and approach
its newly developing ones in an orderly and practical
way.

(2) All the groups should examine certain key elements,
which either in the present structure or in the majority

of alternative models represent clear focal points in the distribution of responsibility and information. These are:

(a) The membership and functions of the Policy Committee;

(b) Standing committees versus ad hoc committees; their membership, functions, and relationship to the total faculty organization.

(3) The present experience should also be evaluated by each group. Each is a heterogeneous, cross-disciplinarian, discussion-oriented committee, without any responsibilities for the ongoing operations of the division and without any specific constituency. Some members have expressed their pleasure at participating in these groups. Others hold a different opinion. The continuing workshop will offer an opportunity to examine the willingness of all faculty members to participate in committee work on a regular basis, and to scrutinize this particular format of "committees" or groups for possible use in the future, either on a regular or occasional basis. Attention should be given to the integration of these "committees" or groups in ongoing operations of the division, to the questions of their membership, and specifically to their possible functions, tasks, powers, and effectiveness.

The following is the Summary from the report submitted in June based on the series of institute sessions:

The faculty workshops in general are recommending a reorganization of the Division of Psychiatry in order to meet the internal stresses created by its own expansion. It is suggested that several general principles or conditions be met in this process:

(1) Delegation of authority and power through decentralization

(2) Development of participatory leadership

(3) Creation of a departmental structure to include all present divisional functions

(4) Establishment of an executive office to assist the chairman

(5) Built-in capability to encompass future divisional functions either by inclusion in existing departments or by adding new departments

(6) Reviews of the committee structure with clear definition of committees' tasks and relationships to the new structure of the division

(7) Review of the committee memberships to avoid repeated assignments of a handful of faculty

(8) Rotation of commitee chairmanship

To achieve these goals we recommend the establishment of a time-limited Task Force to work on the development of a rational model relevant to the general goals of the division.

At the Faculty Meeting of June 25, 1969, the following two motions were passed:

> Moved that the recommendation of the delegates be accepted to establish a time-limited Task Force to work on the development of a rational model, relevant to the structures and functions necessary to achieve the general goals of the Division of Psychiatry (47 in favor, 0 Opposed, 6 abstentions).
>
> Moved that the chairman of the division be requested to appoint the members of the Task Force (28 in favor, 4 opposed, 11 abstentions).

A Task Force under the chairmanship of Dr. Richard Kahn was appointed.

That fall the Policy Committee called a Faculty Meeting, which I was requested not to attend, to discuss the future of the Division of Psychiatry. The following letter was addressed to the Dean of the Medical School by the Policy Committee:

> We would like to express deep concern to you about the unique and critical period of transition now facing us and to make a recommendation about the future of our present chairman, Dr. Bandler.
>
> Cognizant of the fact that he is due to retire in 1970, and aware of the fact that this will be before we move into the community mental health center, the Policy Committee met independently of him and without his knowledge. We shared the feeling that our situation is without parallel: a psychiatric division as strong as any in the country had been built up here, is about to undergo expansion and a period of particular importance since the mental health center involves complex and crucial negotiations and planning with the community. In all of this Dr. Bandler has played a role that could have been played by no one else; he has pioneered an enterprise that itself is new on the national scene. We felt that the whole nature of our program, as well as the outstanding personnel of the division, would be gravely jeopardized if Dr. Bandler were not to continue at the helm of the division during the period of transition into the mental health center.
>
> Accordingly we took a secret ballot and unanimously approved a motion recommending that provision be made for him to continue at the helm during this transitional period.
>
> Our next step was to present a formal resolution to a meeting of the General Faculty of the Division of Psychiatry, again held in Dr. Bandler's absence without his knowledge. This was:
>
> *Resolved.* The faculty in Psychiatry strongly recom-

mends that in view of our unique circumstances Dr.
Bandler continue as Chairman of the Division of
Psychiatry and Superintendent of the Mental Health
Center during the period of our transition into the center.

Seventy-one members were present and voted on the
above resolution. The vote was as follows: *Full-time
faculty*—46 in favor, 1 opposed; *Part-time faculty*—12 in
favor, 2 opposed.

We regard this as overwhelming support for our
sentiments and wish to pass them on for your earnest
consideration.

So here we are in the midst of faculty process. The
Policy Committee is focusing on the principles and
specifics of departmental organization and on the vital
question of sharing power with the community. A drug-
addiction grant now funded was developed in collaboration with Boston City Hospital, Model Cities, Urban
League, FIRST, an indigenous incorporated group of ex-
drug addicts, PLACE, an indigenous South End group
for working with drug addicts, and Puerto-Afro, an
organization of Spanish-speaking people in the South
End. How is power meaningfully to be shared with the
community? We had already developed a successful
model with the Consultation and Education program.
With the drug-addiction grant and the prospect of developing further grants for the staffing of the mental
health center, the implications of our commitment
to the community and of our sharing power with the
community had become more serious and more personal
for all members of the faculty. The faculty will make the
ultimate decision.

The Task Force on Faculty Organization . . . was to report in December, 1969. Although the faculty will decide
on the process to be followed in respect to recommendations of the Task Force, I suspect that the process again
will be that of the workshops. Their recommendations
will then be submitted to the faculty for discussion and
decision.

ACCOMPLISHMENTS AND IMPLICATIONS FOR THE FUTURE

What has been accomplished so far, and what are the
implications for the future? There is, I believe, a greater

sense of community and of cohesiveness. There is also, I believe, a greater sense of participation and of involvement in decision-making. This process of decentralization and participation has also been extended to each of the departments and sections of the Division of Psychiatry. The faculty as an organization is evolving the mechanism for self-government while it and its chairmen are simultaneously working through their mutual separation and loss.

What, then, are the functions and responsibilities of leadership in a democratic, decentralized, participating, and self-governing faculty in its innumerable service, educational, and research responsibilities? Democracy as much as monarchy or authoritarian government requires leadership. The leader has the obligation to think of the department as a whole and to plan for the future in a time of profound professional and social change. His task, among others, is to think of directions and priorities. He does not impose them on faculty; in fact, he cannot in a democratic faculty. Nor would he be successful in an authoritarian structure, since in time the faculty would in its way negate and subvert his endeavors. His power is his strength of vision, his capacity to educate and to persuade, and his capacity to learn from his faculty. He should experience no difficulties in communicating his ideas on education, service, and research to the appropriate structures within the department. He can at least be sure that they will be given an attentive hearing.

For a department to remain viable, I believe it is crucial that it maintain flexibility and possess capacity for innovation and change. The participation of the faculty in decision-making should greatly strengthen a department's adaptive readiness. The responsibility of the leader is to foster, stimulate, and encourage that creativity and change which at the same time conserve continuity.

The question may be asked, why should the chairman's apointment be until his retirement or resignation? Presidents and prime ministers are elected at prescribed intervals. Why should not the faculty periodically elect

its chairman? I know that this is not how medical
schools currently operate in their selection of chairmen.
But institutions do change and can be changed. The
implications of the faculty process as begun in the
institute, it seems to me, would require that the faculty
have the decisive vote in the decision most affecting its
destiny—the selection of its leader. This is true of many
schools where the members of the faculty form a
majority of any search committee selecting a dean.

We live in a revolutionary time where the basic issue in
this country, as we approach our bicentennial, is
whether democracy is to become a reality. For this to
take place requires a profound shift in power, a radical
change in the establishment of which we are part, and a
concomitant change in ourselves. Democracy like charity
begins at home. The Boston institute that was devoted
to community psychiatry initiated the process of democratization of the community of faculty. Both the faculty and I had to change: the faculty to assume responsibility and I to relinquish a benevolent, authoritarian control. It is the essence of process to develop and the nature
of process to be unpredictable. The process continues. I
believe the Division of Psychiatry has been greatly
changed.

We owe a great debt to Drs. Kolb, Bernard, Foley,
Bloom, and their colleagues who were the catalysts and
participants in this process at the beginning. Without
their presence, their commitment, their neutrality—not
in respect to community psychiatry, but in respect to the
feelings of our faculty about the Division of Psychiatry
that exploded about them—I doubt that the process could
have begun. They served involuntarily like so many
trusted analysts in whose presence it was safe to express
emotions and to voice criticisms not possible under the
structure of the Division of Psychiatry. I wonder if one of
the lessons of the institute and of the resulting faculty
process is not the importance of collaboration on the part
of another group trusted as individuals and respected as
colleagues in the initial phases where tensions and
feelings tax the resources of the faculty and threaten its
stability.

We hope that we in turn have contributed to them and through this book to our colleagues throughout the country who may face similar tasks.

6. THE EVALUATION

Samuel W. Bloom, Ph.D.
Sherman Eisenthal, Ph.D.

In keeping with its self-description as an experiment in faculty education, this institute was committed to evaluation from its inception. The definition of the task was similar to Suchman: " ... evaluation research represents an attempt to utilize the scientific method for the purpose of assessing the worthwhileness of an activity. ... The same procedures that were used to discover knowledge are now being called upon to evaluate one's ability to apply this knowledge."[1]

Unlike other uses of the scientific method, however, evaluation research is as much dependent upon administrative considerations as it is upon criteria of validity and reliability. The "success" of an evaluation project, Suchman correctly points out, is largely dependent upon its usefulness to the program administrator.[2] Thus, for the evaluator, scientific considerations do not monopolize the problems of research design: it is equally important to keep his study "simple and practical," and to avoid interfering with ongoing activities.[3]

The evaluation reported here is no exception to the general conditions described for such study. There were practical constraints of time and resources, but balancing these limitations were various advantages. The sincere commitment by the organizers to include evaluation and to protect the independence of the researchers was basic. Equally important to the research was the enunciation, in the stated problem of the institute, of a clear set of objectives. These objectives provide the criterion variables of the evaluation. Moreover, the institute was conceived in terms of educational process and stated in the form of a series of related propositions that can be affirmed or denied on the basis of evidence. The framework for an orderly evaluation is essentially complete.[4]

The recapitulation of the institute's objectives is the first step in this discussion, followed by (2) analysis of the institute participants as a population for evaluation study; (3) a description of the composition of the eight institute discussion groups; (4) the design and methods of the study; (5) a report of the results, subdivided according to (a) predisposing attitudes, (b) general effects of the institute, (c) community mental health ideology, (d) institute groups, and (e) case studies; and (6) a final summary and discussion.

THE OBJECTIVES

The objectives of the institute were stated with specific reference to a problem that Dr. Bandler observed in the teaching and learning of community psychiatry.[5] As he describes it, this is a problem of tension between points of view: the first is the more traditional psychoanalytic approach that, in recent years, has been characteristic of psychiatric residency training; the second is the approach that is called community psychiatry. The tension between these positions, Dr. Bandler believes, is rooted primarily in the lack of full understanding about community psychiatry by the large body of psychiatric faculty who are responsible for psychiatric residency training.

It is not enough for specialists to teach a sub-area like community psychiatry if the broad context in which this teaching occurs is unknowing, suspicious, or hostile to it, Dr. Bandler said. Rather, the disparity between the enthusiasm of a new point of view and the tenacity of a specialty's basic practices tends to force a "polarization" between "those committed to the concepts and practice of community psychiatry and those [who are] committed to the more traditional psychoanalytic approaches."[6]

To reduce such polarization, Dr. Bandler proposed to correct what he regarded as important gaps in the knowledge about community psychiatry in his residency training faculty. The broad general objective of the institute is worded as follows: "A critical problem in training for community psychiatry is *the establishment of a harmonious baseline of knowledge and perspective in the whole faculty.*"[7] The challenge of "perspective," in this statement, refers to a set of predisposing attitudes about community psychiatry that were believed to be present in the Boston University psychiatric faculty and that appeared to dominate the social climate. Only by inducing an intensive social experience focused on the issues of social psychiatry as well as the substances of it as a field would it be possible to engage the participant in the kind of teaching-learning required to effect the desired results. The institute method, centered in a four-day small-group experience, was the method of choice for learning.[8] The presentation of concrete case material, bred of the experience of a respected sister faculty, was the method of choice for teaching.

The institute conceived of its participants (the whole Boston University Division of Psychiatry faculty) as "a community in itself." As such, a four-day "saturation" experience, working together in almost total isolation from the normal distractions of daily routine, was intended as a "tool for sharpening the appreciation of the faculty in respect to community psychiatry by noting and sharing the awareness of the various ways in which the faculty [itself] respond." Moreover, "a workshop provides for the faculty to obtain expert, factual, and clinical information while at the same time having the opportunity to question, agree, and disagree. If conducted as planned, it should also become possible, as a result of the intensiveness of the work and the constant intimacy of the surroundings, to clarify, to a great extent, sources of concern and anxiety that would eventually exert their negative effects in hidden ways upon the future community program and training, including polarization as a major manifestation."

Stated in another way, the more specific objectives derive from a general goal of prevention. The assumption inherent in this formulation is that community psychiatry, as a fact of contemporary life that must be faced by mental health workers, will elicit polarities of commitment and resistance unless these professionals are both informed about its substantive meaning and aware of their own reactions to it. Thus, the specific goals of the institute can be stated within two general categories:

(1) The communication of a body of substantive knowledge concerning specific issues in the field of community psychiatry, drawn, insofar as possible, from existing experience in this area of activity

(2) The uncovering, exposition, and discussion of various attitudes that, as part of the perspectives of psychiatric communities, serve to either obstruct or facilitate the development of community psychiatry

The substantive goals were elaborately specified in two steps. First, twelve categories were listed in the proposal, grouped according to service, training, and research categories.[9]

A second list was extracted from an exchange of letters between the organizers and participants several months prior to the institute.[10] This was initiated by a letter from the organizers outlining the general purposes and requesting each respondent to submit questions and issues that he would like to see discussed at the institute. From the forty-one responses to this letter, another set of content categories was formulated, as given above in Chapter 2, page 21.

There is a considerable overlap between these two lists. It is notable that certain types of social problems, such as poverty and race, were underscored in the participant's responses. There were abstracted from this exchange 132 questions that served as a comprehensive set of guidelines to the interests of the institute participants.

The evaluation that follows will direct its analysis, as specifically as possible, to both lists of content goals. Its main focus, however, is upon the attitudes of the participants.

THE ATTITUDINAL GOALS

The attitudinal problems were conceived with reference to what may be called a problem of revised professional identity formation imposed upon the mental health professions by the current de facto importance of community mental health. This is summarized in the following statement:[11]

> Community psychiatry imposes a new task for psychiatry and for the other mental health professions, namely, the assumption of responsibility for the mental health of a geographical area of the community. This responsibility implies the *extension of the concept of the psychiatrist, a redefinition of his role, the acquisition of new knowledge,* and the development of new *techniques.* [Emphasis added.]

Although it was added that this new responsibility poses both an opportunity and a challenge, in positive terms, the frank emphasis was on its "threat to the identity of the psychiatrist and to all mental health professionals."[12] This threat, Dr. Bandler asserted, can lead to "a defensive reaction" and an associated disparagement of community psychiatry buttressed by arguments that include the following: community psychiatry involves the mental health professional (1) in tasks beyond his professional competence; (2) with responsibilities beyond current knowledge and practice; as a result, (3) residency training for psychiatrists will be diluted; and (4) the psychiatrist will no longer have the expertness that gives him professional identity.

These threats to the more traditional-minded mental health professional were "reinforced," Dr. Bandler stated, by those community psychiatrists who dismiss as outmoded and irrelevant: (1) individual psychodynamics; (2) the dyadic relationship; and (3) the medical diagnostic treatment model.[13]

In the initial formulation of the institute's problem, these were the major attitudinal categories that, it was believed, crystallize into the polarities that divide a community of mental health professionals.

By the time the final meeting of the Planning Committee was held, two weeks prior to the institute, the summary evidence from the Boston University faculty, including the letters from the participants, provided a basis for a more detailed description of the attitude climate within which the institute would begin. As the first step in evaluation, the authors extracted five major attitudinal categories, phrased as problems of value. These were articulated and distributed to the institute faculty as part of the discussion guidelines, as follows:

(1) The problem of *role differentiation versus role homogenization*. This is basically a question of professional identity. Professional mental health workers, particularly psychiatrists, are concerned that the community mental health movement may dilute their basic professional identities.

(2) Intervention under conditions in which patients do not seek professional help. The problem here is one of amplifying the conception of appropriate conditions for professional work to include those most common in deprived communities, where the patient must be stimulated to perceive and accept professional help, as opposed to the traditional conception of the mental health worker responding only when his patient presents self-motivation for treatment.

(3) The questions inherent in *the commitment to social action to change environments*. Community mental health is generally seen, and generally conceives of itself, to include programs designed to achieve environmental change. Mental health workers have several distinct types of concern about such social action:

    (a) The principles for *the selection of action situations*. When is it proper to attempt to initiate social change?

    (b) *The ethical questions* involved in such programs of environmental change. That is, there are complex unknowns in this area that are as great as, if not greater than, those that are very familiar to the individual (one-to-one) psychotherapy situation. What principles, if any, are available to guide the mental health worker in the ethics of such situations?

    (c) Criteria for judging the results.

(4) Problems of *social coercion*. Is community psychiatry committed to activist approaches to a degree that is inherently coercive? What right, if any, does psychiatry have to assume such a moralistic stance?

(5) Problems of *power*. To achieve its goals, is not community psychiatry committed to engage in a power struggle that makes it "political psychiatry"?

There is no doubt that the mood of these questions is defensive. They view community psychiatry as a derivative of administrative problems and therefore as a sub-specialty based on issues of technique, ethics, and social responsibility of substantive knowledge.

For the evaluation, therefore, attitudes were delineated about the role of the mental health professional, the definition of therapist responsibility, the situational elements of legitimate intervention, and the boundaries of professional power as well as patient rights.

THE STUDY POPULATION

An original list of fifty-four invitations grew to include seventy-three formally listed institute participants from the Division of Psychiatry of Boston University.[14] Counting all who attended at least one meeting (two plenary sessions, eight workshop sessions), there were seventy-nine identifiable participants.

Six professional groups were included in the total list of participants, half of whom were psychiatrists and the remainder divided almost evenly between psychology and social work. As shown in Table 1, a small group of nurses and others was included. The original list contained a majority of psychiatrists. The reduction of this majority in the final composition of the institute suggests that a better balance among the mental health professions was deliberately introduced.

Two questionnaires were administered as part of the evaluation study: one just before the institute began, which will be referred to as the "pre-survey"; the second, the "post-survey," immediately upon the completion of the final plenary session. Eighty per cent (sixty three participants) completed the pre-survey, and 67 per cent (fifty-two participants) completed both the pre- and post-surveys.

Failure to respond to the pre-survey shows little or no relationship to occupation. The distribution of the total participants and of the pre-respondents is virtually identical in Table 1. For the post-respondents, the pattern is similar with one exception: the nurses. Only one out of

TABLE 1:
Institute Participants According to Professional Group

Per Cent of Participants

	Originally Invited	Total Participated	Responded to Evaluation Pre-Survey	Responded to Both Pre- and Post-Surveys
Nurses	8%	6%	6%	2%
Social workers	13	19	18	17
Psychologists	20	24	25	27
Psychiatrists	59	47	51	54
Sociologists*	—	2.5	—	—
Public health physician*	—	1.5	—	—
	100%	100%	100%	100%
	N = 54	N = 79	N = 63**	N = 52

* These categories were not differentiated in the original list or the final sample. The sociologists (N = 2) were included with psychologists in the analysis, and the single public health physician was included with the psychiatrists, based on their comparable academic degrees, Ph.D. and M.D.

** One response was only partially filled out so that the pre-survey population is sixty-two on most tables.

the five nurses who were in the total group, and of the four who were in the pre-survey population, persisted and completed the post-questionnaire.

Women participated less actively with each step in the evaluation. As shown in Table 2, less than half of the original number of women participants (thirteen out of twenty eight, or 46 per cent) completed the post-survey; about two-thirds (nineteen out of twenty eight, or 68 per cent) completed the pre-survey. At the same time, fully 86 per cent of the original group of men completed the pre-survey, and 76 per cent completed the post-survey. Thus, as revealed in Table 2, the proportion of women to men shifts from 1 in 3 at the start to 1 out of 4 in the final step of the study.

The sexes are unevenly distributed among the professional groups. Almost all of the psychiatrists who responded to the pre-survey are men, as are two out of three psychologists. The reverse is true for nurses and social workers, as shown in Table 3.

Response to the post-survey does not appear to be related to the sex of the respondent except for the almost complete dropout from the study in the final step by the all-female group of nurses.

On the whole, the respondents are relatively young, with about two-thirds forty years of age or younger.

As would be expected from such a young group, a large majority have been professionally qualified for less than fiften years.

TABLE 2:
Institute Participants According to Sex

Per Cent of Participants

	Total Participated	Pre-Survey Respondents	Post-Survey Respondents
Female	35% (28)	30% (19)	25% (13)
Male	65% (51)	70% (44)	75% (39)
	100% (79)	100% (63)	100% (52)

Chi Square = 1.7496; p is not significant.

TABLE 3:
Sex of Pre-Respondents
According to Professional Group
Per Cent of Respondents

	Psychol- ogists	Psychi- atrists	Social Workers	Nurses
Female	31%	6%	73%	100%
Male	69	94	27	—
	100%	100%	100%	100%
	N = 16	N = 32	N = 11	N = 4
Per cent	25%	51%	18%	6%

TABLE 4:
Age Composition of Study Population
Per Cent of Respondents

Age	Pre-Survey	Post-Survey
Less than 30	16%	10%
30-40	46	54
40-50	27	23
Above 50	11	13
	100%	100%
	N = 63	N = 52

TABLE 5:
Length of Professional Experience of the Study
Population Shown as Years Since Receiving
Professional Degree
Per Cent of Respondents

Years of Experience	Pre-Survey	Post-Survey
Less than 10	42%	39%
10-14	26	29
15-19	10	10
20 or more	22	22
	100%	100%
	N = 62	N = 51

As shown in both Tables 4 and 5, age and length of experience do no influence the rate of response in the post-survey.

Age is unevenly distributed among the professional groups. The psychiatrists are the older, with the social workers and nurses distinctly younger, on the whole. No evidence could be found to show an influence of age upon nonresponse to the post-survey.

Looking at the length of professional experience in each professional group, the pattern for nurses and social workers closely mirrors that of their ages. (Compare Tables 6 and 7.)

Especially for psychologists, the length of time required for training appears to be reflected in the shorter length of their professional experience at similar ages to those of nurses and social workers and, to a lesser degree, in comparison with psychiatrists. In this variable, again, analysis reveals no pattern in those who did not respond to the post-survey.

In summary, the respondents in both the pre- and post-surveys are no different than the total institute participating group according to age, professional group, and length of professional experience. Some difference appears by sex: women are less responsive to the voluntary questionnaire surveys than the men. Typically, the participants were psychiatrists, male,

TABLE 6:
Age Composition of Pre-Survey Population
According to Professional Group

Per Cent of Respondents

Age	Psychologists	Psychiatrists	Social Workers	Nurses
Less than 30	12.5%	—	46%	75%
30-40	69	50%	18	—
40-50	12.5	34	27	25
Above 50	6	16	9	—
	100%	100%	100%	100%
	N = 16	N = 32	N = 11	N = 4

TABLE 7:
Length of Professional Experience in the Study
Population According to Professional Group
Per Cent of Respondents

Years Since Receiving Profession-al Degree	Psychol-ogists	Psychi-atrists	Social Workers	Nurses
Less than 10	57%	23%	55%	100%
10-14	31	29	18	—
15-19	6	10	18	—
20 or more	6	38	9	—
	100%	100%	100%	100%
	N = 16	N = 31	N = 11	N = 4

between thirty and forty years of age, and with less than ten years of professional experience. Considerable variation in this modal pattern exists, however, in the different professional groups and by sex. Thus, analysis shows that the psychiatrists include more older members, with longer experience in their profession. Majorities of the psychologists, social workers, and the nurses have less than ten years of experience. Psychologists, on the other hand, share with psychiatrists a numerical domination by males; the social workers and nurses are almost entirely female.

THE COMPOSITION OF THE
INSTITUTE GROUPS

The eight institute groups varied in size from eight to eleven. As described above (see Chapter 2, p. 20), a committee of the Boston University psychiatric faculty decided upon the composition of these groups. The composition guidelines were profession, known community mental health attitude, the likelihood of attending, and seniority. The intention of the committee was to distribute these selected attributes so as to create heterogeneous groups with at least one favorable

influence as far as community mental health attitudes
are concerned. Selection was guided further by the effort
to avoid clustering the leaders of the various programs of
the Boston University faculty in any one group. It was
anticipated that each group typically would contain four
psychiatrists, three psychologists, two social workers,
and one nurse. These criteria were met very closely in the
final composition of the eight groups, as shown in Table
8.

On other background characteristics, the groups are
less comparable. Groups II, VI, and VII, for example, are
more dominantly male than the others.

In age, one group, VIII, is extremely young, including
no one over forty years of age. Group V, on the other
hand, contains a majority who are over forty.

TABLE 8:
Background of the Eight Institute Groups

Number in Each Group

Background Variables	I	II	III	IV	V	VI	VII	VIII
Profession								
Psychologist	4	1	3	3	3	2	2	2
Psychiatrist	5	4	5	4	4	5	6	4
Social worker	2	3	1	2	2	1	2	2
Nurse	—	—	—	—	1	1	1	1
Sex								
Male	6	7	5	5	6	8	8	5
Female	5	1	4	4	4	1	3	4
Age								
Less than 30	1	—	—	1	1	2	1	3
30-40	4	4	2	3	2	4	4	6
40-50	2	2	3	1	5	2	2	—
Above 50	1	1	1	—	2	1	—	—
N.A.	3	1	3	4	—	—	4	—
Years since degree								
0-10	4	1	1	3	4	4	5	7
11-20	3	3	2	2	2	3	3	2
21+	1	2	3	—	4	2	1	—
N.A.	3	2	3	4	—	—	2	—
Group N	11	8	9	9	10	9	11	9

All but one of the groups reacted favorably to the request that they fill out the post-questionaire. Characteristically, about three-quarters of each group complied; but in one group, only two out of nine cooperated with the final evaluation procedure.

THE DESIGN AND METHODS OF THE EVALUATION

The design of the evaluation was conceived within boundaries set by several practical considerations. The resources were limited, so that parsimony was essential. Perhaps more important, however, was the strength of the organizing group's judgment that nothing should distract from the primary method of the institute: the creation of a total community experience.

Every effort had been made to create a situation where two university psychiatry faculties could freely share ideas about a vital set of issues facing the mental health professions. In the interest of establishing conditions that would optimize the dialogue and promote the most free uncovering of ideas and feelings, the organizers were cautious, perhaps even a bit timid, about allowing anything to intrude that might inhibit the group process. Thus, the evaluation was constrained to be *unobtrusive,* so that it would not change the situation or inhibit the institute interpersonal process; *undemanding,* because the institute participants were busy people who might resent extra demands beyond the institute proper; and *benign,* because of the well-known distaste that people have for inquiry about their own feelings and reactions.

It was decided, therefore, to limit the formal evaluation to a simple before-and-after survey design. To measure baseline characteristics of the participants and their attitudes immediately prior to the institute, a questionnaire was constructed that included measurable scales of community mental health attitudes and required not more than about fifteen to twenty minutes to complete. At the end of the institute, some of the same measures were repeated, in the effort to measure change that was associated with the institute experience. In addition, a number of open-ended questions allowed for more individual accounting and appraisal of what the institute had meant.

Both of the authors were observers at the institute itself. The more qualitative impressions derived from such observation contribute, of course, to the interpretations.

The survey questionnaires are reproduced in the Appendix.[15] Specific measures within these questionnaires will be explained in the context of the subsequent discussion of results.

THE RESULTS

Predisposing Attitudes to Community Mental Health

The general problem of the institute centered about what Dr. Bandler called "tension between points of view." The institute was conceived as a means to decrease polarization for and against the approach called "community psychiatry." The negative position was associated with a "more traditional psychoanalytic" approach. The first question for evaluation tests this assumption. Does the Boston University faculty reveal, in the data available to us, such a polarization of perspective? If it does, are these points of view associated with discernible explanatory variables?

The first source of evidence concerning these questions is the exchange of letters, prior to the institute, between the organizers and forty-one out of the original fifty-four invited participants.[16] The main purpose of this exchange was to elicit questions and problems that the participants wanted to have included in the institute, and, for the most part, the respondents restricted their answers accordingly. On the other hand, some used this occasion to enunciate points of view that support the assumption that the "orientations" described by Dr. Bandler do exist at least in some part. The following two cases are illustrative:

Case 1: A Psychiatrist
Sometimes I have the impression that community psychiatry is a new way of denying the existence of the unconscious.

. . . I am skeptical about the implication that if all psychiatrists devoted themselves to community psychiatry and professional education of lay helpers, rather than spend or waste their time on individual treatment, they could do much more to prevent mental illness.

. . . I seriously doubt that so many more mentally retarded, delinquent, character-disordered, psychotic, and brain-damaged individuals could be helped through community psychiatry and that their occurrence in future generations could be prevented.

. . . I am sure that my comments reflect my lack of sophistication and very likely *my psychoanalytic bias.*

There would seem no reason to doubt that this participant came to the institute with the "traditionalistic, psychoanalytic" orientation toward community psychiatry that Dr. Bandler had concluded was strongly established in a portion of his faculty.

Another respondent wrote a letter with similar assertions and questions:

Case 2: A Psychiatrist
I continue to be unclear about what it is that community psychiatry does, how it does it, or why it does it.

From what I have read and heard, it is my impression that many of the things that community psychiatry does have been going on for a long time so that I do not see why it is considered a separate entity.

. . . I am concerned that community and social psychiatry have already promised more than they can deliver and that there will be an inevitable and harsh disillusionment.

. . . The unique contribution of dynamic psychiatry has been to call attention to intrapsychic factors and their interplay with other components of the personality as well as with the environment. One of the major tasks and difficulties in psychiatric residency training programs is to wean the resident from the action-oriented model in the sense of helping him to understand and help his patients by understanding their thoughts and feelings. The model of community psychiatry seems to shift all the difficulties right back into external reality—an external reality that we as psychiatrists are in no more of a position of knowledge or power to change than anyone else.

Particularly from this respondent's emphasis on "dynamic psychiatry" and his expressed fear of the dilution of the residency training this answer fits together with the first in terms of a predisposing negative orientation to community psychiatry, although the first sounds more extreme.

On the positive side, there were individuals who revealed in their letters a strong sense of both the importance of community psychiatry and an eagerness to learn about it with no evident feelings of guardedness or threat. For example, another psychiatrist (designated as Case 3) wrote:

> The larger question I am concerned with is how to break the cycle of poverty, deprivation, and school failure that characterizes some social groups. . . . Even considering the controversy and unclarity of present knowledge, this kind of information could be of great assistance to the psychiatrist, particularly the child psychiatrist, working in the community who is, of necessity, involved with schools, nursery schools, and social welfare agencies as a consultant and the practitioner who has dealings with schools and agencies in the course of his practice. There is good reason to think that knowledge and programs developed around the questions of major school failure *in large social groups* will also have applicability to the individual problems of school failure in the middle-class youngsters who now already overload child psychiatry clinics and present an increasing problem to society. . . . I will be looking forward to the institute.

The next question is about the whole institute population: Can we say anything about the distribution of similar perspectives as they existed before the institute? If so, what happened to these perspectives? Does the institute measurably influence them?

For answers to these questions, we turn first to the community mental health ideology (CMHI) of sixty-two respondents on the pre-survey, as measured by the CMHI scale developed by Baker and Schulberg.[17] This is a scale of thirty-eight items developed to measure orientation to community mental health. The items are concerned with five conceptual categories:

(1) *A population focus.* The view that the mental health specialist should be responsible not only for individual patients with whom he has contracted for treatment but for the entire popula-

tion of both identified and unidentified potentially sick members in his community.

(2) *Primary prevention.* The concept of lowering the rate of new cases of mental disorder in a population by counteracting harmful forces before they have had a chance to produce illness.

(3) *Social treatment goals.* The belief that the primary goal of treatment is, not to reconstruct the mental patient's personality, but rather to help him achieve social adjustment in an ordinary life situation as soon as possible.

(4) *Comprehensive continuity of care.* The view that there should be a continuity of professional responsibility as the patient moves from one program to another in an integrated network of care-giving services.

(5) *Total community involvement.* The belief that the mental health specialist is only one member of a group of community agents caring for the mentally ill and that he can extend his effectiveness by working with and through other people.[18]

The higher the score on CMHI, the more committed the respondent should be to a community mental health orientation that reflects the above categories of belief. Scores will be reported in two forms: (1) a total score that sums thirty-eight items and (2) a Mean-Item score. Items are scored from 1 to 7, according to a Likert-type intensity of agreement-disagreement. Thus, the highest Mean-Item score possible is 7, and the highest total score is 266; both would reflect the most intense commitment to community mental health ideology.[19]

It should be noted that the use of the CMHI scale did not appear to be popular with the institute participants. Many criticisms of the scale were voiced to the evaluators. Although most of these comments were made directly in conversations at the institute, some were written and provide a vivid record of their spirit. "I doubt very much that my position comes out clearly on so clumsy an attitudinal instrument as the enclosed," wrote one respondent. "Various of the formulations," said another about the CMHI scale, "are so worded as to force distorted or over-simplified responses." One of the psychologists in the group warned about the "test-wise-ness" of most of the institute participants, and questioned the validity of these instruments.

The large response, in view of these criticisms, was encouraging, especially since the survey respondents were asked to sign their questionnaires to allow for deeper data analysis, and participation in the study was entirely voluntary.[20]

The mean score of 219.16 in the pre-survey (Item Mean = 5.765) reveals that the institute group as a whole was moderately favorable in community mental health attitudes as measured by this scale. This relatively high average might be construed as a verification of the "test-wise" assertion, suggesting that the respondents are "dong what the testers are assumed to want." *Does this result invalidate our use of the scale in evaluation?*

The first answer to this question of validity is taken from scrutiny of the survey responses of the three psychiatrists whose letters, cited above, supported Dr. Bandler's assumption of a polarization between a part of his faculty who were, in orientation, negative toward community psychiatry on a traditional psychoanalytic basis and another part who were positively oriented. How do these three respondents score on the CMHI scale? If the scale is valid, it would be expected that the first two would score low in CMHI and the third, high.

Case 1 did not complete the pre-survey questionnaire, explaining the inability to answer a good many of the questions because they were, for this respondent, of the variety of "When did you stop beating your wife?" Insofar as the scale "turned off" Case 1 and produced a nonresponse, there is reinforcement for the argument against the validity of the CMHI scale.

However, Case 1 *did* respond to the post-survey, including the CMHI scale, scoring in the low range (99–180)[21] but at the top boundary. (Case 1 CMHI score = 180.) This datum will be analyzed further below.

Case 2, the second psychiatrist discussed above as an individual example, completed both pre- and post-surveys. His CMHI pre-score was the lowest recorded in the sample: 99, or a mean-item score equal to 2.605. In the specific terms of the scale, he is in moderate disagreement, for the most part, with the attitude statements representing the favorable community mental health ideology. Moreover, unlike Case 1, he had no apparent difficulty answering the questions: he took a neutral stance on none of the items, and on eighteen items was in strong disagreement with community mental health ideology. As will be shown, this is a very low score in comparison both with the norms reported by the authors of the scale and in comparison wth his Boston peers. In at least this single case, therefore, the CMHI scale accurately reflects an orientation toward community psychiatry insofar as two independent measures of the same set of attitudes coincide (the pre-institute letter and the CMHI scale).

The third psychiatrist, Case 3, scored 210 in CMHI (Mean-Item score = 5.526), which is in the middle of the distribution. Similarly, two other letters that expressed clearly favorable general orientations to CMHI were compared with CMHI scale scores: one was 246, or in the high range of scores and the other was 214, in the middle range.

These data comparing the pre-institute letter and CMHI scale scores are not in any way definitive tests of validity. On the other hand, they offer some support that the scale discriminates among community mental health points-of-view.

Further evidence of the construct validity of the CMHI scale may be derived from the question that asked each respondent how strongly he identified with each of four psychiatric orientations: (1) somatic (organic); (2) psychotherapeutic; (3) sociotherapeutic (milieu); and (4) community mental health. Total score on the CMHI scale was significantly correlated ($r = .57$, $p < .01$) with self-rating of degree of identification with a community mental health orientation. There was also a significant correlation ($r = .29$, $p < .05$) between CMHI scale score and identification with a sociotherapeutic orientation, in keeping with the general conception that community mental health includes the elements associated with a sociotherapeutic approach. A psychotherapeutic self-orientation correlated negatively (r = minus .23) as did the somatic orientation (r = minus .01), but neither of these latter relationships is statistically significant. The pattern of these responses is generally the same as that reported by Baker and Schulberg.[22]

If we accept, for the moment, the validity of the CMHI scale, what, more specifically, does it tell us about the institute participants that relates to the evaluation variables?

In general, the psychiatrists are the least favorable among the various professional groups in their attitudes toward community mental health. On the other hand, they are slightly more favorable than a sample from the American Psychiatric Association. (Boston University Mean CMHI scale score = 208.57, standard deviation [SD] = 37.59; American Psychiatric Association = 198.93, SD = 37.02.)[23] The Boston University social workers have the most favorable CMHI scale scores (Mean CMHI = 228.78, SD = 15.26). Again, the pattern of comparative response is the same as that reported by the authors of the scale in their report of criterion group data.

On analyzing each of the CMHI variables separately, we find that the institute participants on the whole, regardless of background and professional affiliation, share the belief that there should be a "comprehensive continuity of care" and "total community involvement," as those categories of belief are defined above.[24] On sixteen of the items in the pre-administration of the CMHI scale, a very high congruence of beliefs is shown by item averages of six or more. This means that, typically, there was a moderate to strong agreement favorable to community mental health on all of these sixteen items for the whole institute. Almost half of these items (seven) concerned comprehensive continuity of care, and five others were concerned with issues of total community involvement. The only category that was not represented at all by a favorable consensus was "social treatment goals."

The item that invoked the most disagreement was the following: "12. Our program emphasis should be shifted from the clinical model, directed at specific patients, to the public health model, focusing upon population." In other words, the institute population, for the most part, was still committed to the traditional clinical model of individual psychotherapy at the time that the institute convened.

The widest diversity of opinion, involving the most equal split between agreement and disagreement, occurred on the following item: "2. Our time-tested pattern of diagnosing and treating individual patients is still the optimal way for us to function professionally."

Item-by-item analysis thus indicates that commitment to the goals of *comprehensive care* and *community involvement* is the most universal. Issues involving the traditional methods of mental health treatment, the *how* and *what* of the problem, elicit the greatest division of opinion, including a strong segment that seeks to preserve the psychotherapeutic model. The view that argues for extending the mental health specialist's focus from the individual patient to populations-at-risk invokes some general consensus, and so does primary prevention. However, the latter attitudes are apparently much less crystallized than the agreement with concepts of comprehensive care and community involvement.

Data from the Semantic Differential Scale[25] follow a similar pattern to the CMHI scale. A large majority of the participants came to the institute with conceptions of community mental health as timely, important, and needed; as relevant but complex. On none of the adjective-dimensions were majorities negative in their attitudes, but many respondents (33 per cent or more) regarded it as weak and naive. About 20 per cent regarded conceptions of community mental health as "ineffective." A large minority also judged it to be "conflicting" rather than "cooperative."

The psychiatrists were the most negative on the Semantic Differential Scale and the social workers the most positive, just as they were on the CMHI scale, but the differences were not statistically significant.

Another and more surprising finding in the analysis of pre-institute attitudes suggests that the more one teaches, the more negative his attitudes toward community mental health. This is indicated first by a small, but statistically significant, negative correlation between CMHI and the allocation of time to teaching ($r =$ minus .34 $p < .01$). None of the other functions (administration, consulting, research, supervision, treating patients) are correlated significantly with CMHI. The same type of negative relationship appears between teaching and the attitudes measured on the Semantic Differential: on fourteen of the nineteen dimensions, the more one teaches, the more likely he is to be negative toward community mental health.

Summarizing the evidence about the attitudes prior to the institute, there is some support for the assumption that polarization had occurred in the Boston University faculty toward a negative feeling about, and resistance to, community mental health concepts. As assumed by the institute organizers, these attitudes appear to be based on a commitment to the importance of the psychodynamic approach and the feeling that this approach is being diluted by a new focus that is of lesser functional value professionally. On the other hand, some modifications of the earlier formulations about this polarization are also indicated.

On certain community mental health concepts, there is broad favorable consensus; on others, the differences are indeed sharp. The data of the pre-survey provide information to specify these areas of agreement and difference.

Recalling the attitudinal dimensions that were believed to be polarized, they included mainly the following: (1) the role of the mental health professional; (2) the definition of therapist responsibility; (3) the situational elements of legitimate intervention; and (4) the boundaries of professional power as well as patient rights. According to the data presented, it would appear that the issues of professional role and responsibility are the most critical for our respondents. Questions of professional legitimacy, power, and patient rights are less vital. The hard lines of polar differences, therefore, seem to form primarily around the questions of *who is the mental health specialist* and *what exactly is the type and range of his responsibilities?* Once these questions are answered, our respondents seem to be saying, the distribution of rights and authority between the professional and his patient will be resolved.

The General Effects of the Institute

On the basis of observation alone, it seems justified to say that the general effects of the institute were favorable; that, for virtually all involved, the experience had been stimulating and meaningful. The data of the post-survey support this impression. Fully 91 per cent reported favorable effects in their *understanding* about community mental health; 70 per cent *approved of the format* of the institute; the small groups were rated very high for their *over-all excellence* and the *intelligence of the discussion;* and negative change in attitudes was virtually absent from the otherwise extensive comments about the institute that appeared in the post-questionnaire. More detailed analysis, however, raises important questions about the more specific effects.

The attitudinal effects, to begin with, are substantially more problematic than those involving knowledge. The latter are documented in Table 9, suggesting that the substantive or knowledge objectives of the institute were, at least in some general sense, achieved with a high rate of success.

TABLE 9:
Agreement That the Institute Added to
Understanding of Community Mental Health*

Answer to Question**	N	Per Cent
Definitely *yes*	26	51%
Qualified *yes*	21	40
Qualified *no*	2	4
Definitely *no*	3	5
	52	100%

* This variable will be referred to below as "Knowledge Change."
** The question was: "Did this institute add to your personal understanding of community mental health? If it did, what kinds of information and understanding were most meaningful to you?"

Concerning the attitudinal objectives, on the other hand, the data are quite different. Only 49 per cent believed that their attitudes were changed in a favorable direction (Table 10).

Very few, it should be noted, felt a negative attitude change, but almost half reported *no* change. Is it possible, then, that there was an entrenchment of existing attitudes? To what extent was it the people who began with negative attitudes who experienced a reinforcement of their point of view?

To answer these questions, several different kinds of data will be considered. First, there are CMHI scale scores, providing a comparison of predisposing attitudes with those measured by the same instrument after the intervening experience of the institute. Secondly, predispositions as measured by the pre-survey CMHI scale can be studied according to the knowledge change and attitude change that respondents reported as self-perceptions in the post-survey. Finally, the meaning of trends in these data is explored through the detailed statements of individual cases.

TABLE 10:
Subjective Estimates by Participants Concerning Whether Their Attitudes Were Influenced by the Institute

Whether and How Attitudes Were Affected*

	N	Per Cent
Strong positive change	3	7%
Moderate positive change	4	9
Slight positive change	15	33
No change	21	47
Slight negative change	1	2
Moderate negative change	1	2
Total answered	45	100%
No answer	8	
Total N	53	

* The question: "Have your attitudes been affected by this institute? If so, how?"

Community Mental Health Ideology

Telescoping the pattern of findings, the CMHI scale data indicate that those who came to the institute with strong value positions concerning community mental health, whether positive or negative, maintained substantially the same positions, relative to their professional colleagues. However, those who are in the middle range of measured CMHI crystallized their attitudes in both directions, but more toward the positive. There is also evidence that for both those who start with negative attitudes and those who start with positive attitudes, notable change occurs in a positive direction.

None of these trends appear from gross score comparisons, but they do become clear in the before-after panel analysis. Thus the average scores of the total sample are virtually identical on both the pre- and post-surveys: the pre-institute Mean CMHI score = 215.48, SD = 31.14, and range = 99–261; the post-institute Mean CMHI score = 217.27, SD = 31.72, and range = 145—266. The same general lack of change is observed among the professional groups, as shown in Table 11.

Only when the individuals are studied, as in the matrix of pre- and post-CMHI scores shown in Table 12, do patterns of attitude change emerge.

TABLE 11:
Scores on Community Mental Health Ideology (CMHI) Scale in Pre- and Post-Surveys According to Professional Group

| | CMHI Scale Mean Scores* | | |
	Psychologists	Psychiatrists	Social Workers
Pre-survey	218.86 (SD = 36.24)	208.56 (SD = 37.56)	228.78 (SD = 15.26)
Post-survey	220.00 (SD = 31.33)	209.57 (SD = 36.24)	225.67 (SD = 25.40)

* No significant differences in table.

TABLE 12:
Matrix of the Pre- and Post-Institute CMHI Scores

Pre-Workshop	Post-Workshop			
	Low	Me-dium	High	Total
Low (99-180)	6	0	0	6
Medium (181-220)	3	12	6	21
High (221-266)	0	0	25	25
Total	9	12	31	52

All of the low scorers (N = 6) on the pre-survey remained low scorers on the post-survey. The increased number of low scorers on the post-survey (N = 9) is explained by three respondents who scored in the middle range in the pre-survey. The increase from twenty-five to thirty-one high scorers, as shown in Table 12, similarly is explained entirely by shifts from the medium range. Thus, out of twenty one who scored initially in the medium group, only twelve remain, with the largest number (N = 6) changing into the high category.

Stated most succinctly, the pattern in Table 12 is for change of attitude to occur *only* among the scorers of the middle range; no categorical shifts occur among the pre-survey low scorers or among the high scorers. In effect, this challenges what is perhaps the most basic objective of the institute: the reduction of a polarization of orientations toward community mental health. The suggestion in this matrix is that the institute acted to consolidate the extremes and polarize the uncertain in their attitudes toward community mental health. *Is this actually what happened?*

In seeking to answer this type of question, we find that the statistical rendering of the data is more meaningful when combined with a case method. Case study makes it possible to explore in depth the available information about individual subjects who are selected for scrutiny from among types of response that are statistically defined. Using this method, we find that the matrix of pre-post CMHI scores disguises some rather dramatic individual changes. The psychiatrist whom we earlier referred to as Case 2, for example, was the lowest scorer in the pre-survey (CMHI = 99). He then scored 50 per cent higher (more favorable to community mental health) in the post-survey (CMHI = 146), but his post-score places him again in the low category in Table 12. Quite clearly, it is false to interpret this as a "consolidation" or reinforcement of his negative attitudes toward community mental health. On the contrary, he has been influenced to what appears to be a modification of his extreme position, a result that is exactly the depolarization effect that was intended by the institute.

Looking at the post-CMHI scores of all those who begin in the category of low scorers in CMHI, we find that three subjects (one is Case 2) improved their attitudes toward community mental health, two register lower scores, and one has an identical score. When pre-survey CMHI scores are analyzed with reference to the respondents' subjective estimates of how the institute affected their attitudes (Table 13), the pattern of change is more complex than the pre-post comparison of CMHI scores shown in Table 12 and more like that revealed from the more precise panel analysis of each individual's scores.

TABLE 13:
Subjective Estimates of Attitude
Change According to Final CMHI Score (N=52)

Attitude Effect*	CMHI Score		
	Low	Medium	High
Strong or moderate positive change	—	2	4
Slight positive change	2	6	7
No change	2	8	11
Some negative effect	—	1	1
No answer	2	4	2
Total	6	21	25

* See Table 10 above for explanation of this variable. Chi Square is *not* significant.

From these data, the conclusion that there was at least some depolarization effects by the institute gains credibility. At all levels of CMHI scale score (low, middle, high) change occurs in a positive direction (as perceived by the respondents concerning their own attitudes). Very little change occurs in a negative direction.

Knowledge change, on the other hand, does show some relationship to attitudes as measured by the CMHI scale. "Knowledge change" is defined here (see Table 9) as a variable based upon the question that asked whether the institute added to the respondent's personal understanding of community mental health. Any indicated change is therefore positive. Table 14 shows how subjective estimates of knowledge change are related to CMHI scores.

High CMHI scorers show a notable (though not statistically significant) tendency to say that the institute definitely increased their understanding of community mental health; low CMHI scorers do not.

The full implications of these data about community mental health ideology require further interpretation. Before continuing, however, analysis of the institute process, as represented particularly in the eight discussion groups, is inserted at this point.

TABLE 14:
Knowledge Change According to Final CMHI Scale Score (N = 52)

	CMHI Score		
Knowledge Change	**Low**	**Medi-um**	**High**
Definitely *yes*	1	9	16
Qualified *yes*	4	8	9
Qualified or definite *no*	1	4	—
Total	6	21	25

Chi Square = 8.1740; $.05 > p < .10$; compressing the cells to correct for small expected frequencies yields same values for p. It is *not* significant.

The Institute Groups

In explaining the institute effects on both knowledge and attitudes, the experience in the eight discussion groups is, according to the planned structure of the institute, a critical determining variable. In the analysis so far, we have been concerned mainly with the measurement of the attitudes of the participants, before and after the institute, seeking to find the nature and patterns of change. The intervening institute experience was focused in the discussion groups.

To measure the reaction to the discussion groups, a Group Rating Scale was developed by the evaluators, derived from a small-group process scale constructed by Kostick.[26] This is a twenty-one-item scale in which respondents rated various aspects of group functioning. For each item, the range of score is 1 to 7,* as in the following example:

Discussion was:

    intelligent 7 6 5   3 2 1 dull

In this particular item, the higher the score, the more favorable the reaction to the group's actual behavior and functioning. Each rating item must be treated separately in this discussion because the total instrument has not been tested and validated as a single scale.

As shown in Table 15, there was a very favorable overall rating of the group function (Item 21). This confirms the reactions to the post-survey question concerning the

---

* The instructions were as follows: "*Purpose:* The purpose of this rating sheet is to measure your perception, *as a group member,* of how your workshop group functioned. Please rate the *actual* behavior that was expressed in the group by drawing a circle around the number that seems to be the position of the group. Notice that the scale has statement 'A' on the left and statement 'B' on the right. You are to select numbers 1 to 7 according to your agreement with the statements as follows:

7—Practically all statement A, not statement B
6—Very strongly statement A, very weakly statement B
5—Slightly more statement A than statement B

3—Slightly more statement B than statement A
2—Very strongly statement B and very weakly statement A
1—Practically all statement B and not statement A"

TABLE 15:
Overall Means and Analysis of Variance of Group Rating among Eight Discussion Groups

	Statement "A"	Statement "B"	Mean Score	F
1.	Worked intensely	Worked relaxed	5.073	< 1
2.	Held a high standard	Compromised	5.473	1.13
3.	Dominant leadership	Without leadership	4.891	< 1
4.	High commitment to problem	No personal commitment	5.982	< 1
5.	High production of ideas	Low production of ideas	5.309	2.01
6.	Worked at fast pace	Got bogged down	4.782	2.73*
7.	Was physically restless	Sat motionless	3.527	< 1
8.	Members tended to seek personal recognition	Members sought understanding of others' ideas	2.473	< 1
9.	Cordial exchange of ideas	Impersonal exchange of ideas	5.673	< 1
10.	Concern for group unity	Not concerned with group unity	3.891	1.39
11.	Warm and intimate	Formal and objective	5.309	< 1
12.	Emphasis on theory	Emphasis on concrete	3.891	1.21
13.	High concern for details	Low concern for details	3.582	< 1
14.	Organized and on course	Discussion wandered	4.491	1.26
15.	New ideas encouraged	New ideas resisted	5.509	1.73
16.	Discussion easy-going and calm	Discussion emotional	4.364	6.73**
17.	Open conflict	Conflict ignored	4.745	3.77**
18.	Deference shown	No special treatment given	3.218	< 1
19.	High concern for rules	Discussion free and spontaneous	2.127	2.69*
20.	Discussion was intelligent	Discussion was dull		
21.	Over-all rating excellent	Over-all rating unsatisfactory	5.655	3.62**

* Significant at .05.
** Significant at .01.

TABLE 16:
Reaction of the Participants to the Format of the Institute

Comment*	N	Per Cent
Strongly favorable	18	41%
Moderately favorable	12	27
Slightly favorable	1	2
Neutral	4	9
Slightly unfavorable	2	5
Moderately unfavorable	4	9
Strongly unfavorable	3	7
	44	100%
No answer	8	
Total	52	

* The question: "As freely as possible, and from your own personal view, would you comment on the format of the institute. What, if any, aspects were highlights? Were there unexpected events, content, or problems? What, if anything, would you have liked to see done differently?" The coding in this table concerns the first part of the question.

format of the institute, on which fully 70 per cent commented favorably (Table 16).

When the groups are compared, however, important differences are discerned. Specifically, there are significant differences among the eight groups for the general ratings of function (Table 15, Items 20 and 21) and about perceptions of emotionality (Item 16), conflict (Item 17), degree of structure (Item 19), and pace (Item 6).

In their over-all ratings,* the members of two groups were clearly very pleased with the way their groups functioned. One group was strongly negative; the other groups were moderately favorable. There is no identifiable relationship between the demographic variables of age, sex, and professional experience (variables in which unequal distributions among the groups were found to exist) and general reaction to the group process.

Approval of the format of the institute is *not* associated with attitudinal predisposition as shown in the

* To protect the promise of anonymity of individual responses, it is not possible always to identify each group in discussion of the data about the variations among the groups.

CMHI scale or the Semantic Differential. Moreover, a favorable group rating of the institute is not necessarily associated with positive changes in the group's average CMHI scale score: in some groups it was, in others it was not. The more strong negative group responses were associated with a decline in the group's Mean CMHI score. (See Figure 1.)

Neither group ratings nor attitude changes were explained by the participants' reactions to the question about the coverage of important issues. Almost all respondents agreed that *the important issues were discussed* and "adequately treated."

The more intensively one analyzes these data about group process, the more individualized the "effects" appear to be. Although there are indications that some groups produced a significantly stronger sense of élan, a kind of small-group *esprit de corps,* individuals within both the "successful" and "unsuccessful" groups made their judgments on quite different bases, and reacted in patterns of "effects" that our data do not explain in terms of social facts. Thus, Cases 1 and 2 (as we identified them in the above discussion) are sharply critical of the general format of the institute, yet both thought the discussion in their groups covered the important issues. They also gave high ratings to the intelligence of the discussion in their separate groups (Table 17).

Because the implications of these various findings are elusive without further study of the full statements of selected respondents, we turn again to the cases cited in depth above.

Case Studies

Case 1, it will be recalled, is a psychiatrist with very strong negative views about community mental health, expressed in a variety of specific doubts and skepticism, candidly associated with "psychoanalytic bias." Concerning the institute's influence upon understanding, Case 1 responds with an unequivocal "no," explained as follows:

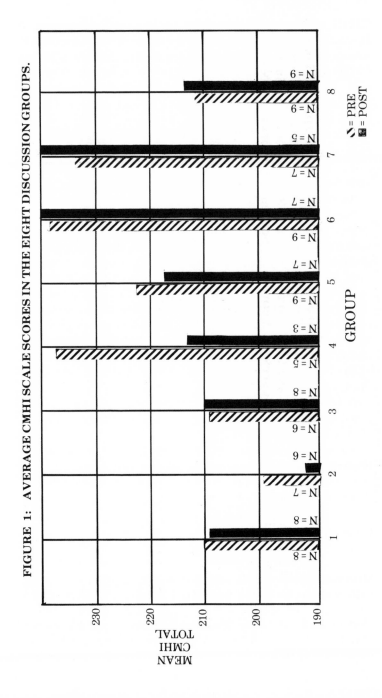

FIGURE 1: AVERAGE CMHI SCALE SCORES IN THE EIGHT DISCUSSION GROUPS.

TABLE 17:
Group Rating Scale Scores of Selected Cases and Their Groups

Group Behavior Stated in Brief	Case 1 Scores	Group of Case 1, Mean Scores	Case 2 Scores	Group of Case 2, Mean Scores	Mean Scores of Total Post-Survey (N = 52)
1. Worked intensely—relaxed	3	5	6	6	5.07
2. High standards—compromised	3	5.57	5	5.33	5.47
3. Leadership—without leader	2	4.71	5	4	4.89
4. High commitment—none	5	6.14	6	5.66	5.98
5. High production of ideas—low	5	5.42	5	4	5.31
6. Worked fast—bogged down	3	4.28	3	3.83	4.78
7. Physically restless—not	3	3.57	3	3.83	3.52
8. Sought recognition—understanding	3	2.42	1	3.17	2.47
9. Cordial idea—exchange—impersonal	6	5.42	6	4.5	5.67
10. Group unity—none	2	3.71	2	2.63	3.89
11. Warm—formal	5	5	7	5	5.31
12. Theoretical—concrete	6	4.57	6	4.33	3.89
13. Detailed—low	3	3.42	2	3.5	3.58
14. Organized—not	2	4.28	3	4.5	4.49
15. New ideas—resisted	6	5.42	5	4.66	5.51
16. Discussion calm—emotional	5	5	3	2.66	4.36
17. Open conflict—ignored	3	4	6	6.63	4.74
18. Deference—none	6	3.43	5	3.66	3.22
19. Concern for rules—free	1	2	3	3	2.13
20. Discussion intelligent — dull	5	5.42	6	4.63	5.73
21. Over-all excellent—unsatisfactory	3	5.25	5	4	5.66

> I do not think that the institute added to my personal understanding of community mental health, which remains in my opinion a very nebulous, semi-conceptional, and semi-operational term.
>
> ... There seems [to be] a great deal of confusion as well as overlap between the use of community mental health, community psychiatry, preventive psychiatry, and social psychiatry. It was most reassuring to me to find that my own knowledge and awareness were not as antiquated as I feared and that I had applied many techniques and principles without being aware that I was practicing something new and different. I was disappointed by the fact that so much confusion and fuzzy thinking still seems to dominate this field. Also, I was impressed by the great emphasis on doing and a lack of a well-conceived conceptual framework that could serve as a ground plan for organizing and steering the various activities.

Attitudes , however, are a different matter from knowledge change for Case 1, who reports a slight positive change of attitude, prefaced by the opinion that negative attitudes toward community mental health are widespread in the Boston faculty:

> I think that I share with many members of the Boston University Division of Psychiatry my objections against what at times seem random action, poor planning, and tendencies to do the possible right away and to assume the impossible will just take a little longer. My attitudes have been affected by the institute insofar as I was impressed by the resourcefulness of our resource consultants who brought quite innovative ideas based on excellent thinking and purposeful planning. I would like to mention as an example Dr. Bard's work with the New York police.

Turning to Case 2, we find a quite different result. Indeed, the effects are reversed. He reports a definite increase of understanding but no change in his attitudes. Concerning understanding, he states: "The institute did add to my personal understanding in presenting a range of activities that are subsumed under the title (community mental health), but more especially that this is a structure—with functions to be added—rather than a series of techniques."

Answering the question about attitudes and how they had been affected by the institute, Case 2 answers with a story:

Once upon a time, I went to college. I arrived there with a willingness to learn but also as a product, to some extent, of previous experience. In my third year, I took a course in philosophy taught by a superb and knowledgeable teacher. My views concerning the philosophy of religion did not coincide with his, and we saw eye-to-eye about very little. I emerged from the course, however, with a clearer idea of why he thought the way he did, although I disagreed with his conclusions and still do.

This institute has been a somewhat similar experience for me. I can see more clearly what some of my colleagues think. I see also that there is a wider division (in terms of both numbers and issues) than the chairman thinks, but my basic position about community psychiatry is unchanged.

At any rate, I continue to number myself with those who are not enthusiastic about community psychiatry.

The cases selected to represent favorable letters (Cases 3 and 4, both psychiatrists) also, like their negative-minded colleagues, give quite individual responses. Case 3 did *not* think he "learned much," but he did gain in understanding because "problems were focused" and "logistics, tools" were clarified. Case 4 was more generally favorable in his reaction (as he was in CMHI scale score), giving special credit to Boston University: "Hearing and meeting with members of our Division of Psychiatry was a welcome and quite educational experience. We are doing some exciting things here and need more intercommunication."

Concerning the institute effects on attitude, Case 3 says "yes" (slightly), Case 4 takes a slightly negative view, but at the same time, he praises his discussion group.

Case 3

I think my attitude was affected to the extent that I am now clearer about both the intent and the problems faced by this approach.

Case 4

My attitudes have been changed by the institute in the following way: I now feel that the frenetic pace, work over-load, and lack of communication within the division are forcing people to take stands along the continuum (of community mental health attitudes) rather than to cooperate more effectively. I was impressed with the goodwill, community spirit, and desire to work together seen in our group.

Concerning the format of the institute, both the negative and positive cases are critical, on very varied bases. Case 1 wanted more structure; Case 2 preferred greater informality and more free expression of attitude. Case 3 was more enthusiastic about the Boston participants than the "so-called resource people." Case 4 itemized both pluses and minuses. In their own words:

Case 1

It was my impression that there were certain inconsistencies in the way in which the institute was set up. Most of us had come with the notion that we wanted to hear and learn as much as possible. This went somewhat against the other aim of the institute that seemed to have to do with the development of group interaction and group problem-solving. Personally, I felt that these double aims were apt to defeat rather than to enhance each other. I would have preferred a more structured and definitely informative program rather than a free-for-all that I felt at times was very frustrating to our resource person.

Case 2

In our group there was a misunderstanding about the institute right from the beginning. The group leader thought that discussion should revolve around the presentations of the resource people. Many of us in the group had been told repeatedly that the purpose of the entire institute was that it be an expression of attitudes and feelings and a confrontation with issues. We did get to issues, but not as much as I would have liked.

I think it would have been better to have informed the participants (or even asked them in advance) of the proposed format and even have tailored it to the expressed wishes or needs. The format had too much of a fait accompli about it and not enough grass-roots participant collaboration—a strange position for a department that prides itself on community participation. (Except when it comes to its own faculty? I don't know.)

Case 3

I enjoyed the institute and its format. The experience of getting to know the group was the best part for me. The resource people were not as helpful (to me) as was the general exchange of ideas. The group already had people of wide and varied experience. The so-called resource people had little more and were felt to be either outsiders or intruders.

The main problem was having the institute held at home where other duties interfered with regular attendance and slowed down the progress.

Case 4

(1) Sunday night was a bomb!

(2) Our group leader and our discussions were excellent.

(3) The general air of secrecy about the planning of the conference was resented by myself and others.

(4) The format on paper was excellent.

(5) It was important that our leader knew when to temporarily shunt aside the resource person when he noted the group's desire to confront intradivisional problems.

(6) Rumors of breakdown of confidentiality in the Training for Teaching questionnaires to residents affected many people in confronting these evaluations.

(7) It was unavoidable but unfortunate that we couldn't have met away from Boston. I personally missed the opportunities for informal discussions.

(8) I think the planners skirted narrowly the input overload in this conference. Holding workshops in the evening after a full conference is antithetical to orderly development of concepts and more in keeping with our department's crisis philosophy.

Cases 3 and 4 were coded "favorable" in their comments, while 1 and 2 were both unfavorable.

Summarizing the case presentations, we find that beginning with two individuals with negative predispositions about community mental health, the institute produced quite different types of effects. Understanding and attitudes, in these cases, vary independently of each other. Thus, Case 1 reported no increase of understanding but a change of attitude, whereas Case 2 reacted precisely in the reverse.

For the two cases who began with favorable attitudes, the reported effects were also quite varied. Both singled out their Boston colleagues for special praise. Neither reported major effects on either understanding or attitude; they emphasized a "clarification-effect." Case 4 found that polarization of attitudes among colleagues was deeper than he had known, but he felt that "goodwill" was a balance. The format impressed both favorably in conception, but they were critical of its operation, especially with reference to the site (they preferred that the institute be held "away from home") and the way some of the resource people functioned.

Space does not allow the review of these qualitative data in their full richness. There were, for example, enthusiastic reports to balance the more critical reactions of the selected cases above. The following are some of the responses to the question concerning understanding: "Yes! The over-all view by the numbers of problems . . . was depressingly and challengingly impressive." "The techniques and social points of the resource people—notably Dr. Bard, Mrs. Jeffers, Dr. Newman, and Dr. Bernard—were highly interesting for me." "The shared experiences of two colleagues . . . were illuminating and encouraging. I got to know them better, and increased my already flowering respect and admiration." "The forced necessity to try to think through my own priorities was helpful and unsettling."

The complexity and richness of these case reports dramatize the limitations of the various survey instruments used in this evaluation. The institute was concerned with an extraordinarily complicated issue that evokes subtle but important tones of variation in basic attitude and in the effects of the institute itself. Nevertheless, the patterns that are extracted from the survey techniques, though less textured than the individual reports, tell us a great deal.

FINAL SUMMARY AND DISCUSSION

In a final assessment, what can be said—following Suchman's injunction to the evaluator—about the "worthwhileness" of the institute? In attempting to answer this question, we will shed, for the moment at least, the constraints of the formal data and speak freely about some impressions.

There was a spirit and mood to the institute that eludes precise description but that the participants invariably reach for when asked to comment. Its essence, in our judgment, was drawn primarily from the Boston University community itself rather than the organized program and structure of the institute. Most intensively, it was from each other, between one Boston colleague and another, that meaningful learning (and teaching) occurred. In this conclusion we are not downgrading the contribution of the visiting faculty: on the contrary, their presence and their contributions were essentially to draw together and motivate the Boston University members to invest their attention and energies in this extraordinarily concentrated experience. Once the commitment was actualized, however, the direction of the group process turned inward. Each of the eight small groups quickly achieved, sometimes in easy harmony and sometimes in more conflictful struggle, an intimacy that was essentially parochial. If there was a hidden agenda, it was this rather violent demand for "communication," and although community mental health was the excuse, the issues ranged far beyond. Always, however, the boundaries of concern for action were local, and the search of inquiry was toward each other.

In this setting, the faculty and resource people were guests or, more precisely, strangers. The Boston University colleagues quickly set about the business of discovering things about each other, and the surprise and excitement of discovery produced an impatience with any interruption to the natural flow of relationships in the small groups. There were exceptions, of course. The psychiatrist whom we discussed above as Case 1 is one who "preferred a more structured and definitely informative program rather than a free-for-all. ..." In the main, however, it was the "grass-roots participant collaboration," as Case 2 phrased it, that was sought and preferred.

If we are correct in this first general conclusion, the choice of format was indeed felicitous. The institute method, as it was specifically intended in Dr. Bandler's original formulation, achieved its goal of "inducing an intensive social experience."[27] The focus of this experience, however, was not, as designed, concentrated in community mental health. Community mental health functioned more as a point of departure for the emergent social experience than as its core subject.

What, then, was the focus? We have only hinted at the character of the mood and behavior of the institute, and have not touched its underlying themes. To be sure, the outer form of this behavior is remarkable enough to preoccupy one's whole attention. Here were a group of co-workers, in a setting that is not generally considered to be extreme in its urban anonymity or anomie, and who are part of a university medical school that is relatively small and contained. Yet, they reacted passionately to this opportunity for drawing closer together, as though a sample of intimacy in their work lives were a missing but essential ingredient.

In effect, what began as an "institute for training in community and social psychiatry" became a potential revolutionary marking point in the life history of the Boston University Division of Psychiatry. Such seemingly far-removed questions as the division's authority-structure, definition of constituency, and methods of governance came forcefully to the surface and became the major sustaining concerns of the follow-up meetings that resulted from the institute. But what do these outcomes mean? Are there any explanations for this swift and deep interpersonal involvement, the hunger for personalized work relationships, and the demand for participatory decision-making that emerged in the meeting?

It is tempting to conclude that the pattern of attitudes in this special group of professionals is a mirror-image and a reflection of the general climate of challenge and dissent that pervades the greater community. There is a familiar ring to the charge that the division, as it has grown rapidly larger, has become more bureaucratic, extending and attenuating the lines of communication among its members. The onus is softened somewhat by calling this problem an undisputed product of "success," but, in the report of the follow-up workshop, six months later, the evils assigned to modern bureaucratization are stated clearly:

> Seen from the point of view of many members of the division, uneasiness manifests itself as a feeling of a lack of participation in the life of the division. This ranges from relative isolation to fairly strong—yet suppressed—feelings of not being consulted and informed adequately in the processes of making decisions that affect their professional lives and that require their participation.
>
> . . . seen from the point of view of the development of the division, the challenge is very much the basic one of coping with the extraordinary success and growth of the division, under the peerless leadership of Dr. Bandler. . . .[28]

The outer form of the complaint is clear enough, but what are the "decisions" concerning "professional lives" that are causing so much anxiety? The answer, we believe, is found in the attitudes, shown in our data, that the participants brought with them to the institute.

The state of mind that our data describe is one of role uncertainty. A crisis of professional identity appears to have been triggered by the emergence of pressure upon the mental health professions to give higher priorities to the problems of community mental health than ever before. Dr. Bandler, the highest authority in the Boston University Division of Psychiatry, has accepted this assignment with alacrity and has worked vigorously to implement it. The members of the division share his dedicated concern for the social problems of the community and the implications in the mental health of the population. Our data show that the goals of community mental health are not at issue. The confusion centers about the question of *who* does *what* to achieve these goals.

More specifically, the concepts of *comprehensive care* and *community involvement* are widely accepted by the Boston University professional group. No serious questions are being raised about the continuity of professional responsibility, about the need for an integrated network of care-giving services, and about the belief that "the mental health specialist is only one member of a group of community agents caring for the mentally ill and that he can extend his effectiveness by working with and through other people."[29]

The issues of power, legitimacy, and patient rights—all of which appeared highly significant at the time the institute was conceived—proved to be relatively *in*significant among our respondents in comparison with issues of professional role responsibility and behavior. Especially among the psychiatrists, these problems of professional identity appear to be matters of vital concern.

Up to this point, it has been possible to speak of mental health specialists as one group, but further specification of the problem separates the psychiatrist from his professional collaborators. It is the psychiatrist who clings most doggedly to the traditional psychotherapeutic model as the guiding frame-of-reference for his professional behavior. This model is not claimed to be transferable to community problems ("the cycle of poverty, deprivation and school failure"—as cited by Case 3 above); but, the psychiatrist asserts, it is "what we can do" and "what we can teach." It is the hallmark of "what we are." The abstract knowledge and clinical skills of psychodynamic practice provide a coherent structure for professional identity, and it is against these secure certainties that community and social psychiatry is perceived as vague and unspecific in both basic knowledge and skill.

Nor are the psychiatrists' nonphysician collaborators separated from the psychodynamic model. The clinical psychologist and social worker, for example, have by and large accepted this dominant professional ideology in the recent past. In the main, previous challenges have occurred only with regard to fine points of doctrine and technique—not with regard to whole patterns. This is not the case for community psychiatry, which poses what can be interpreted as a more far-reaching type of challenge. At least, this is the perception of our respondents. For the psychiatrist, the challenge is the most fundamental and the most threatening.

In fact, for the collaborating professionals, the uncertainties of the community mental health movement are offset by the promise of increased status. The physician is defending a model in which his superiodinacy is secure. For the collaborating (nonmedical) professionals, the cry for more communication and participation may well be part of a thrust toward more power by the achievement of equal status on the mental health team. The psychiatrist is not vulnerable, as it were, to such a distraction from what he considers the basic questions of what is most valid in both knowledge and skill. He, therefore, takes the stance of the defender of the known against the unknown, whereas his colleagues, though no less uncertain about the verities of the new movement, are more eager to engage and consider the possibilities.

This brings us to our final question: to what extent did the institute achieve what it set out to achieve?

The first part of our answer has already been stated: namely, that there did occur, as intended, an intensive social experience within which a kind of immersion in the issues of community mental health took place. That this process served to reduce the polarization between points of view that Dr. Bandler described is less clear. Some depolarization was indicated in our analysis, but, among strategic figures in the Boston psychiatric community, the evidence suggests that reinforcement of extreme attitudes may have occurred.

On the other hand, an unforeseen consequence of the institute was the establishment of new structures for the purpose of continuing the institute process. If some polarization was deepened, therefore, a method was introduced to prevent anyone from resting easy in established positions.

Of one thing there is no doubt: the institute was an intensely vital experience for all the participants. This is revealed by the emotional feel developed *at* the institute *about* the institute.

REFERENCE NOTES

1. Edward A. Suchman, *Evaluative Research: Principles and Practice in Public Service and Social Action Programs,* New York: Russell Sage Foundation, 1967, p. 20.

2. *Ibid.,* p. 21.

3. *Ibid.,* p. 22.

4. *Ibid.,* pp. 30-31. The requirements for evaluation research are thoroughly reviewed here by Suchman. "Identification of the goals to be evaluated" is the first step always.

5. Several closely related terms are used in this chapter, particularly "community psychiatry," "social psychiatry," and "community mental health." To avoid confusion, they are defined as a field of practice (community psychiatry), a field of inquiry (social psychiatry), and the goal of these fields (community mental health). The first two terms are explained and differentiated by Viola W. Bernard, "Education for Community Psychiatry in a University Medical Center," in Leopold Bellak, ed., *Handbook of Community Psychiatry and Community Mental Health,* New York: Grune & Stratton, 1964, Chap. 4, pp. 83-122. Community mental health is a generic conception of what the full range of professions that are involved in these fields (community psychiatry and social psychiatry) are seeking to achieve.

6. Bernard Bandler, "The Need for Faculty Education in Training

Facilities," from "Workshop—Faculty Education in Community Psychiatry," NIMH Grant Application No. MH-9540-01 August, 1967, p. 2. Emphasis (italics) is added by the evaluators.

7. *Ibid.*, p. 6.

8. Speaking of the various methods that are being used, on a day-to-day basis, to build a community mental health point of view in the Boston University faculty, Dr. Bandler lists: (1) the clinical problems relevant to their natural setting; (2) reading and discussion; (3) activities and preparation for the Boston University-Commonwealth of Massachusetts Community Mental Health Center; and (4) consultation to community facilities. These methods and experiences help, he states, but they are not enough. "They lack intensity, depth, and the concentrated margin of time necessary to saturate one's self in the subject. Textbooks on community psychiatry and regional workshops for professors of psychiatry do not give an opportunity for the members of faculty who actually work together to subject their questions, doubts, uncertainties, and outright opposition to mutual examination and solution with experts. A well-conceived plan of faculty education in community psychiatry must not only include the wealth of factual information already available as literature but also take full cognizance of the needs of a group of professionals who are, by tradition, independent; who tend generally to move slowly in new directions; and, most importantly who are themselves a community." (See Bandler, op. cit., pp. 14-15.)

9. See Bandler, op. cit., p. 15. The categories may be restated as follows:

A. Service
    (1) Conducting a service program
    (2) Program planning and development
    (3) Mechanisms of coordination in community mental health work
    (4) Principles of consultation of various types

B. Training
    (5) Residency training
    (6) The principles of concomitant treatment in interprofessional personnel (not just the old child-guidance team)
    (7) The principles of new alignments of professionals and new coordinations of services with accountability and responsibility

C. Research
    (8) Research generally (the relevance of particular questions for which investigation would be a guide to action)
    (9) The integration of psychodynamic, group dynamic, administrative, and social-process perspectives
    (10) The operations of individuals and groups from different segments of relevant social reality
    (11) The multideterminance of community mental health and community action from different levels
    (12) Program evaluation

10. These procedures are described in detail above in Chap. 2. Their brief recapitulation here is only for clarification of the framework of evaluation.

11. Bandler, op. cit., pp. 13-14.

12. *Ibid.*, p. 14.

13. *Ibid.*

14. See list, "Participants in the Institute."

15. See Appendix C, "Pre-Institute Questionnaire" and "Post-Institute Questionnaire."

16. The letter sent by the institute organizers and the responses are discussed in Chap. 2 above, pp. 20-21.

17. Frank Baker and Herbert C. Schulberg, "The Development of a Community Mental Health Ideology Scale," *Community Mental Health Journal,* 3: 216-225, 1967.

18. *Ibid.,* p. 217.

19. As explained by Baker and Schulberg, the items were arranged "in Likert format with provision for respondents to circle one of six response categories for each item: strongly, moderately, or slightly agree; and strongly, moderately, or slightly disagree. On positively worded items, strong agreement is scored 7; moderate agreement, 6; slight agreement, 5; slight disagreement, 3; moderate disagreement, 2; strong disagreement, 1. Reversed scoring is used for negatively worded items. When no response is given, a score of 4 is given to that item." *Ibid.,* p. 218.

20. There were sixty-two usable CMHI scale responses in the sixty-three returns from the pre-survey (78 per cent of the seventy-nine total institute participants) and fifty-two who completed both pre- and post-surveys (67 per cent of the total). The procedures used insured anonymity in the response by giving responsibility for coding and for any necessary identification of respondents to one of the evaluators (SWB) to be retained entirely outside of Boston University and unavailable to anyone and for any purpose except for essential analysis of data.

21. This group of low scorers is defined as more than one standard deviation below the over-all Mean CMHI score.

22. Baker and Schulberg, op. cit., p. 222.

23. These and subsequent comparative scores are drawn from Baker and Schulberg, op. cit., pp. 221-223.

24. Above, pp. 133-134; and *Ibid.,* p. 217.

25. The scale used is the same as Herbert C. Schulberg and Frank Baker, "Varied Attitudes to Community Mental Health," *Archives of General Psychiatry,* 17:658-663, 1967, derived from the method described by C. E. Osgood, G. J. Suci, and P. H. Tannenbaum, *Measurement of Meaning,* Urbana, Ill.: University of Illinois Press, 1957.

26. M. M. Kostick, *Rating on Group Effectiveness,* Brookline, Mass.: Applied Psychology Associates, 1966.

27. Whether it would have been more effective at a site removed from Boston is questionable. This was the institute's original plan, to meet at Arden House, as some participants suggested in retrospect. On the other hand, having met in Boston may have provided a sense of continuity with the follow-up meetings that were requested and successfully implemented—continuity that might not have been achieved with an Arden House meeting precisely because of its separation from the *in vivo* quality that pervaded the meeting in Boston.

28. Report (issued on January 28, 1969) by the Committee of Delegates of the meeting of eight groups at the December 11, 1968 Workshop of the Faculty of the Division of Psychiatry, Boston University School of Medicine, p. 2.

29. Baker and Schulberg, op. cit., p. 217.

7. COMMENTARY: REFLECTION ON THE OVER-ALL INSTITUTE EXPERIENCE

Viola W. Bernard, M.D.

The Boston University institute stands out as one of the most challenging and disquieting and at the same time reassuring and stimulating occasions I have experienced during the course of a long involvement in community psychiatry. Some of the reasons for this will emerge, I think, as I reflect back on the institute as a whole.

I shall not attempt a systematic review of this remarkable enterprise, which has, after all, been covered by the preceding chapters. My outlook vis-a-vis the institute was of necessity from the Columbia University side of "The Dialogue." But the multiplicity of my roles and responsibilities throughout all its phases, to which Dr. Foley has already referred, afforded me an overview of the entire institute process. It is from that vantage point that these comments are offered.

The institute process began, for me, when Dr. Bandler first broached the idea in May, 1965 and invited the Columbia University Department of Psychiatry, through its Division of Community and Social Psychiatry, of which I was the director, to help plan, organize, and conduct such an educational venture.* The three

* The Division of Community and Social Psychiatry at Columbia University is under the joint auspices of the Department of Psychiatry and the School of Public Health and Administrative Medicine of the College of Physicians and Surgeons. To avoid confusion, the reader should keep in mind that the term "Division" for the Columbia group refers to a component of the "Department of Psychiatry," which is headed by Dr. Kolb, whereas Boston University's "Division" (of Psychiatry) corresponds to the "Department" of the College of Physicians and Surgeons of Columbia University.

years that elapsed between that initial conversation and the point at which the institute became a reality were packed with dynamic developments relevant to community mental health; these developments took place not only within the field of psychiatry and its related disciplines but also in each of the two medical schools, in their adjacent communities, and in the social and political climate at large.

It is not surprising, therefore, that when we accepted Dr. Bandler's proposal with enthusiasm and confidence—after discussions involving Dr. Kolb, Dr. Foley, the other divisional faculty members, and myself—we did not foresee much of what, in actuality, the institute came to involve. By the time it was to take place, the scene had changed in so many ways that, while I was still enthusiastic about the prospect of an intensive discussion with respected colleagues, I felt considerably less clear than earlier about what we as a "visiting faculty" could offer in such a situation. On one point, however, we were very clear: we were not going as missionaries, intent on converting skeptics to a "community psychiatry movement," nor with the expectation of providing answers to the unanswerable; instead, our aim was to share experiences, ideas, and viewpoints toward problem-solving in the complex tasks of rendering psychiatry more effective in serving community need.

Indeed, the need for differentiated designations—"visiting faculty" for the group from or assembled by Columbia University and "participants" for Boston University faculty members—was a source of some discomfort to both the host group and the visitors. Its hierarchical connotations ran counter to the mutuality of interchange that the institute was seeking to achieve. I believe that such mutuality did prevail, however, largely as the result of the professional maturity on the part of all concerned, which overcame certain hazards in this respect that were inherent in the institute design. Among these hazards was the existence of some discrepancy between an "Interfaculty Dialogue" concept of the institute and the fact that the two groups were, in various ways, not symmetrical enough to fit into such a concept, at least as it is usually understood. Thus, there was the numerical preponderance—about fourfold—on the part of the Bostonians. But there were also important differences of purpose and function between "faculty" and "participants." The Columbia group (actually, this is something of a misnomer, in that several of the resource consultants and one discussion leader, though recruited by us, were from other faculties) had responsibilities toward the Boston University faculty that were not reciprocal. Our mission, generally speaking, was to function primarily on behalf of the Boston division's interests and goals; in that sense, there was of necessity an imbalance to the "dialogue." In fact, this led some of us in the Columbia group to envy our Boston colleagues for the very opportunity to which we were contributing: greater communication among themselves in grappling with the problems that concerned them; and we wished that some of them, in turn, would provide our faculty back home with a comparable occasion, for which we felt a very great need.

The reason for this is that one of the drawbacks of community psychiatry has been the extent to which pressures for speedy action have tended to crowd out the time that a group so engaged might otherwise devote to joint reflection. This need on the part of "those who work together to reflect together" cannot be met by the many different kinds of national or regional institutes and conferences mentioned earlier in this book. Of course, such interchanges have been of immense value in the general development of community psychiatry and community psychiatrists; but the very participation in these, for some of us, has been an added reason for our being too busy to meet with our own co-workers—except for day-to-day immediacies—so as to think through and work through the specific issues, conflicts, and feelings that are most closely bound up with our own programs. Inevitably, these programs suffer, and feelings of overwork, isolation, self-doubt, and frustration are all the more likely to burden one's approach to community mental health work.

THE INSTITUTE'S OVERRIDING
VIRTUE

Accordingly, the overriding virtue of the Boston institute, for me, was the setting aside, by an entire faculty, of
a number of days in which to discuss with each other,
through small-group discussion, the hard issues, new opportunities, and problems of professional importance to
them at a time of institutional and social change.

The idea of including in these deliberations a selected
core of colleagues from outside their own ranks and,
further, of entrusting them with key responsibilities was
an intriguing invention, which of course gave rise to a
wide range of reactions before, during, and after the institute. A picture of how this invention worked took shape
as one read the foregoing accounts of each institute
group, in terms of both content and process, along with
the impressions of each discussion leader and resource
consultant, Dr. Bandler's illuminating discussion of an
ongoing faculty process of change at Boston University,
set in motion by the institute, and the evaluation by Dr.
Bloom and Dr. Eisenthal.

Both Dr. Bloom and Dr. Bandler have emphasized
those functions of the visiting group that pertained not
so much to community psychiatry per se but to the specific interests and needs of the Boston University faculty
members in relation to each other and to their own institution. Thus, Dr. Bandler has noted that "two agenda
were at work simultaneously in the institute process: the
manifest, overt agenda of community psychiatry; and
the latent, covert agenda of the democratization of the
[Boston University] Division of Psychiatry." In characteristically generous terms, he credits the Columbia
group, in regard to this latent agenda, with fulfilling a
catalytic role without which he "doubts that this process
could have been begun."

The visiting faculty did, of course, need to recognize
"the feelings of the Boston faculty, which exploded
around them," as Dr. Bandler puts it, and to make on-the-
spot adjustments to these feelings by modifying our own

role functioning, as we went along, in the service of this highly charged intradivisional process.

But this should not obscure, I believe, the extent to which the institute's participants were in fact deeply occupied with the manifest agenda of community psychiatry. Since this was, after all, the basis for our presence there, the visiting faculty felt obligated to adhere to its original mandate with regard to the institute's overt aims. The chapters on Content and Process and on Faculty Reflections reveal, I think, how much the institute sessions did indeed focus, through earnest and high-caliber discussion, on the most salient and timely issues of community psychiatry. The several mechanisms for maintaining feedback that were built into the institute design proved to be very useful to the faculty's effort to help maintain balances between the two agenda.

DAILY REVIEWS OF INSTITUTE SESSIONS

One of these mechanisms was provided by what was, for me, a fascinating and important ingredient of the total institute process. As Dr. Foley has mentioned, all the discussion leaders and resource consultants joined with me, at the end of each day, to review each of the institute sessions of that day. The sharing of these accounts while the institute was in progress enabled us to attune ourselves more sensitively to each group as its special characteristics emerged. A discussion leader would report on the content and process of his group's sessions, including transactions between himself and the group, between the morning and afternoon consultants and the group, and between the consultants and himself. As each resource consultant in turn reported on the same sessions, as observed and experienced from the standpoint of his role, we could better understand what was going on, catch our own and each other's mistakes, and devise improvements. These meetings also strengthened faculty morale by enhancing the sense of group unity, cohesion, and support that arose among us.

Although the transcriptions of these tape-recorded sessions contain a wealth of insightful material, to include

them in this book would make for too much repetition. As
a source of data, however, these accounts, when studied
in conjunction with those prepared by the recorders and
discussion leaders, provide a stereoscopic picture—and a
moving picture, at that—of each group's functioning. A
comparable effect is achieved by combining the data on
each faculty member's experience, as developed horizon-
tally in these daily faculty meetings, with their subsequent impressions, as presented in vertical form in
Chapter 3. The meshing of these several sets of data
makes for a fuller and more accurate understanding of
the institute as a whole.

THE INSTITUTE'S DEFECTS IN RETROSPECT

Of course, with hindsight, one can always find various
shortcomings and mistakes. The planning group, for instance, had apparently erred about the extent to which
the Boston University faculty felt they had participated
in the planning process. (Our pre-institute efforts to elicit
and heed their agenda suggestions did not, in my judgment, wipe out the various resentments about decision-
making that Dr. Bandler has described.) Many of us felt
that a conference center setting, as originally sought,
with its opportunities for informal mingling and
personal exchanges, would have improved matters
greatly, especially in view of the tensions and the hunger
for communication that prevailed. Instead, the workshop
sessions, which were the only occasions for interaction,
were overloaded, in terms of all that they had to accomplish. Probably this was one of the factors in the under-
utilization of resource consultants that was mentioned
by several participants.

Nor should it be overlooked that the community psychiatrists at Columbia were also caught up in "the revolutionary times" to which Dr. Bandler has referred in connection with the Boston division. The Columbia campus
violence had erupted a month before the institute, with re-
percussions both at the Medical Center and in our division. We were in the midst of hostile confrontations over

the community mental health center toward which we had been working for years. Looking back, I realize that the stresses and pressures that these and related crises entailed for me at that time must surely have had some effect on how I carried out my institute responsibilities. I think this contributed, for example, to the reasons why the plenary session and its case presentation on that first night failed to work out as intended.

But the very fact that the institute took place at a time of turmoil was its most compelling reason for being. Many of the visiting faculty, including myself, not only felt that we learned a great deal from and with our Boston colleagues, but also derived profound encouragement from the quality of shared commitment and fundamental values. This is not to deny the presence of tensions and disagreements, which were clearly in evidence. They too are essential to the evolving of creative solutions. But it was the transcending spirit of the occasion that strengthened our mutual confidence and respect, and we are grateful to Dr. Bandler and his associates for bringing this institute into being.

APPENDIX A

INITIAL LETTER TO PARTICIPANTS

December 20, 1967

Dear

Dr. Bernard Bandler has submitted to us your name as a participant in the Institute for Training in Community and Social Psychiatry which is to take place at Boston University in June of 1968. We would appreciate your letting us know which areas or issues, in particular, relevant to the field of community and social psychiatry you would be interested in having covered at the workshop sessions of the institute.

We would like to have your reply by January 15, 1968 so that we can develop a meaningful program for presentation at the institute.

Sincerely,

VWB:ARF:pk

LETTER TO INSTITUTE FACULTY

March 2, 1968

Dear

We are extremely pleased that you are going to be able to participate as a member of the faculty for the Institute for Training in Community and Social Psychiatry to be held in Boston, June 9-13, 1968. We have been meeting with Dr. Bernard Bandler, Professor of Psychiatry at Boston University, over the past months and are now in a position to talk somewhat more definitively about the format and content of the institute.

176

In order to involve the participants, that is, the faculty of the Division of Psychiatry of the Boston University School of Medicine, in the process of planning the institute, we have written and asked them to let us know what issues they would like to have discussed during the four-day workshop. We are sending you a summary of their responses, outlining the issues and content areas that they would like to have discussed. The number in parentheses after certain questions indicates the number of times this exact question was asked.

The first page of this summary is a list of fourteen headings that have been thought to encompass a number of questions raised. It is our feeling, then, that these will be the issues that will be most discussed, although other issues almost certainly will be raised. In addition, we are sending you a portion of the original application to NIMH for sponsorship of this experiment in faculty education. These pages describe the need for such an institute, as seen by Dr. Bandler, and the basic philosophy from which this institute has evolved.

The institute will follow the small-group format, each group meeting twice a day and being composed of seven or eight members of the Boston University faculty with a group leader who will stay with the group throughout the four days and one resource person who will rotate from group to group whenever that group is discussing his special area of expertise. Plenary sessions will be kept at a minimum since it is felt that our goals can best be achieved through small-group interaction. For Sunday evening, a plenary session is scheduled with a presentation to help pinpoint some of the issues in community and social psychiatry and which will serve as a jumping-off point for discussion the next morning. In this way, it is hoped that the participants will be involved in the work of the institute immediately upon their arrival. There also may possibly be a plenary session on Thursday afternoon to wind up the institute.

We will be in touch with you from time to time during the next few months to ask your advice and to pass on whatever further information we might have available. It may be necessary to have a meeting of the faculty for the institute sometime before the start of the institute, and we will be in touch with you about this at a later time.

May we ask you to send us an updated curriculum vitae which will be included with advance material we will circulate to the participants prior to the institute. We do want to involve the participants in planning for the institute as much as we can, and we think this is one way of acquainting them with the participating faculty. We would also appreciate your specific suggestions as to advance material to be sent to the participants or recommended readings.

We thank you for helping us out and we will be in touch with you again, soon.

Sincerely,

VWB:ARF:pk

SECOND LETTER TO PARTICIPANTS

April 19, 1968

Dear

We want to thank you for your response to our inquiry concerning the issues that you would like to have discussed at the forthcoming Institute for Training in Community and Social Psychiatry, to be held June 9-13, 1968. You and your faculty colleagues have indeed given careful consideration to formulating your replies and have raised many pertinent issues that need to be aired and shared, which we hope will take place at the institute.

We are sending you a summary of the replies that we received, listing the various questions asked, and, in parentheses, after the question, the number of times the exact same question was asked.

The format of the institute will be that of small-group discussions, meeting morning and afternoon throughout the four days. The groups will be composed of seven or eight members of your own faculty, selected in consultation with Dr. Bandler and Dr. Mann, and two resource people, one of whom will act as discussion leader and remain with the group for the four days, while the other resource person will visit each group for one session.

We would like your opinion on how best to utilize the evenings. Sunday evening there will be an opening presentation to set the stage, so to speak, for the small-group discussions for the next few days. Tuesday evening will be free. The institute will terminate late Thursday afternoon and, therefore, our question to you relates to how we might best make use of Monday and Wednesday evenings.

It might be useful to shift the emphasis for these two evenings to the resource people and, in that case, the following are possibilities:

(1) Continue the daytime group composition, but have selected resource people available at the request of the group.

(2) Have each resource person set up shop, so to speak, so that the participants meet, in re-groupings with the resource person who best meets individual areas of interest. Another alternative, of course, is to have all three evenings free.

Would you please let us know your thoughts on this, as well as any other ideas you might have about the format or content of the institute.

Sincerely,

VWB:ARF:pk
Enclosure

APPENDIX B

RECOMMENDED READINGS

Each resource consultant and discussion leader was asked to submit several readings he considered relevant to his special area. To assure time and availability for each participant to study the recommended material, the list was limited and some copies were made available and some of the shorter papers were circulated to participants.

Recommended by C. Knight Aldrich, M.D.

British and American Psychiatry. *Journal of the Kansas Medical Society,* January 1965, 66, 11-15.

Impact of Community Psychiatry on Casework and Psychotherapy. *Smith College Studies in Social Work,* February 1968, 38, 102-115.

The New Approach: Intervention and Prevention—The Clinical Psychiatry Model. *The Social Service Review,* September 1966, 40, 264-269.

Recommended by Elizabeth B. Davis, M.D.

Harlem Psychiatric Unit Marks Second Anniversary. *The Bulletin,* New York State District Branches, American Psychiatric Association, October 1964, 7, 1-6.

———, Lerner, B., & Raskin, R. On the Need to Be Pregnant. *International Journal of Psycho-Analysis,* 1967, 48, 288-297.

The Clinical Practice of Community Psychiatry at Harlem Hospital. *Journal of the Hillside Hospital,* 1968, 17, 3-12.

Recommended by Sheldon G. Gaylin, M.D.

Psychiatric Planning at the Community Level. *American Journal of Psychiatry,* February 1964, 121, 153-159.

An Inventory of the Clinic Patient Load in a Community Mental Health Program. *American Journal of Public Health,* December 1965, 55, 1909-1924.

———, et al. Data Utilization for Local Mental Health Program Development. *Community Mental Health Journal,* January 1967, 3, 30-32.

Recommended by Ruth G. Newman, Ph.D.

———, with Long, N., & Morse, W. *Conflict in the Classroom.* Belmont: Wadsworth, 1965.

Psychological Consultation in the Schools: A Catalyst for Learning. New York: Basic Books, Inc., 1967.

———, & Kieth, M. M. (Eds.). *The Life Space Interview.* Washington School of Psychiatry, 1963.

The School: The Effects of an Institution in Infantalizing Students and Staff. Mimeographed.

Recommended by Marvin E. Perkins, M.D.

Some Antecedents of Mental Health with a Look Forward. *Medical Annals of the District of Columbia,* January 1961, 30, 13-18.

The General Hospital: Local Agency for Community Mental Health Services. *The Psychiatric Quarterly Supplement,* January 1963, 37, 111-118.

Facilities and Functions (Fitting Care to Patients' Needs) Hospital and Clinics. *Journal of the Hillside Hospital,* April 1964, 67-68.

Relationship of the Psychiatric Unit to Municipal and State Hospitals. *The Psychiatric Unit in a General Hospital,* M. Ralph Kaufman (Ed.). New York: International Universities Press, Inc., 1965, 442-450.

Mental Health in Relation to Agency Mission. *The Psychiatric Quarterly Supplement,* Part I, 1965, 39, 95-109.

Recommended by Alex Richman, M.D.

————, & Tyhurst, J. S. Psychiatric Care in a General
Hospital. Presented at the Annual Meeting, American
Public Health Association, Miami Beach, Florida,
October 1962. *Canadian Hospital,* May 1965, 42,
45-48, 90.

Psychiatric Care in Canada: Extent and Results, a
study prepared for the Royal Commission on Health
Services, Ottawa, 1964, Queen's Printer, 1966.

Assessing the Need for Psychiatric Care: A Review of
the Validity of Epidemiologic Surveys. *Canadian
Psychiatric Association Journal,* November 1966,
179-188.

Recommended by Maurice V. Russell, Ed.D.

A Study of Factors Influencing Academic Achievement,
a pilot study of graduate students at Columbia University (1950), requested by Dr. Hans Rosenhaupt,
Director of Graduate Admissions, Columbia University.

A Community Mental Health Program in a Municipal
Hospital. *Social Casework,* November 1965, 46, 557-
560.

Mental Illness in Negroes. *The Crisis,* December 1966,
73, 520-524.

Recommended by Alvin M. Mesnikoff, M.D.

————, with Spitzer, R., & Endicott, J. Program Evaluation and Planning in a Community Mental Health
Service. *Psychiatric Quarterly,* March 1967, 41, 405-421.

The Effects of the Establishment of a Community Mental Health Service on Residency Training. *Journal of
Medical Education,* October 1958, 43, 1059-1067.

Effects of the Mental Health Project on the Psychiatric
Institute. *Urban Challenges to Psychiatry: The
Case History of a Response,* L. C. Kolb, V. W. Ber-
nard, & B. P. Dohrenwend (Eds.). Boston: Little,
Brown, 1970.

Recommended by Leonard Siegel, M.D.

Live Supervision in Multiple-Impact Therapy. Paper presented at the William Alanson White Graduate Seminar on the Supervisory Process, Winter 1965. Mimeographed.

Family Psychodynamics of School Avoidance in Adolescence. Paper presented at panel, School Phobia and School Avoidance in Adolescents, New York Society for Adolescent Psychiatry, May 17, 1967. Mimeographed.

System-Changing Family Experiences in Conjoint Family Psychotherapy: Targets and Tactics. Panel, Family Psychotherapy: Strategy and Techniques, Fifth Biennial Division Meeting, New York State District Branches, American Psychiatric Association, New York, November 17, 1967. Mimeographed.

Recommended by Samuel W. Bloom, Ph.D.

Rehabilitation as an Interpersonal Process. *Sociology and Rehabilitation,* Marvin Sussman (Ed.). Washington: American Sociological Association, 1966, 114-131.

The Doctor and His Patient: A Sociological Interpretation. New York: Free Press, 2nd Ed., 1965, paperback.

The Sociology of Medical Education: Some Comments on the State of a Field. *Milbank Memorial Fund Quarterly,* February 1965, 43, 143-184.

Recommended by Viola W. Bernard, M.D.

Some Aspects of Training for Community Psychiatry in a University Medical Center. *Concepts of Community Psychiatry: A Framework for Training.* Bethesda, Maryland: U.S. Department of Health, Education, and Welfare, 1965.

Some Principles of Dynamic Psychiatry in Relation to Poverty. *American Journal of Psychiatry,* September 1965, 122, 254-267.

————, with Crandell, D. L. Evidence for Various Hypotheses of Social Psychiatry. *Social Psychology,* J. J. Zubin & F. Freyhan (Eds.). New York: Grune & Stratton, Inc., 1968, Vol. 24, Proceedings of the American Psychopathological Association.

Recommended by A. R. Foley, M.D.

————, Glasscote, R. M., Sanders, D., & Forstenzer, H. M. *The Community Mental Health Center: An Analysis of Existing Models.* Washington: The Joint Information Service of the American Psychiatric Association and the National Association for Mental Health, 1964.

————, with McKinley, D. A., Jr. Case Study A: A Metro-Suburban-Rural Community Mental Health Center. *Architecture for the Community Mental Health Center,* Coryl L. Jones (Ed.), Houston: Rice University and Mental Health Materials Center, Inc., 1967.

Current Trends in Community Mental Health. *Proceedings of the Staff Training Institute,* of the National Association for Mental Health, Miami Beach, Florida, June 17-21, 1963.

Caplan, Gerald. Conceptual Models in Community Mental Health. January 1968. Mimeographed.

Riessman, F., Cohen J., & Pearl, A. *Mental Health of the Poor: New Treatment Approaches for Low Income People.* New York: Free Press, 1964.

T-Group Therapy and Laboratory Method. *Innovation in Re-Education,* L. P. Bradford, J. R. Gibb, & K. D. Benne (Eds.). New York: John Wiley & Sons, Inc., 1964.

Towle, Charlotte. *Common Human Needs.* New York: National Association of Social Workers, Rev. Ed., 1965, paperback.

National Advisory Commission on Civil Disorders. The Commission Report. Washington: U.S. Government Printing Office, April 1968.

Edwards, George. *The Police on the Urban Frontier,* Pamphlet No. 9. New York: American Jewish Committee, 1968.

Niederhoffer, Arthur. *Behind the Shield.* New York: Doubleday & Co., Inc., 1967.

Group for the Advancement of Psychiatry, Committee

on Preventive Psychiatry. *The Dimensions of Community Psychiatry,* Report No. 69. New York: April 1968.

Hughes, Charles C., et al. Chapters V & VII. *People of Cove and Woodlot.* New York: Basic Books, Inc., 1960.

Cumming, John, & Cumming, Elaine. *Ego and Milieu: Theory and Practice of Environmental Therapy.* New York: Atherton Press, 1966, paperback.

Stanton, A. H., & Schwartz, M. S. *The Mental Hospital: A Study of Institutional Participation in Psychiatric Illness and Treatment.* New York: Basic Books, Inc., 1954.

Pavenstedt, E., et al. *The Drifters: Children of Disorganized Lower-Class Families.* Boston: Little, Brown, 1967.

Sarason, S. B., et al. *Psychology in Community Settings.* New York: John Wiley & Sons, Inc., 1966.

Handbook of Community Psychiatry and Community Mental Health, Leopold Bellak (Ed.). New York: Grune & Stratton, Inc., 1963.

Gladwin, T. Social Competence and Clinical Practice. *Psychiatry,* November 1967, 30, 30-43.

Coles, Robert. *Children of Crisis: A Study of Courage and Fear.* Boston: Atlantic-Little, Brown, 1967.

Caplan, Gerald. *Principles of Preventive Psychiatry.* New York: Basic Books, Inc., 1964.

Hollingshead, A. B., & Redlich, F. C. *Social Class and Mental Illness: A Community Study.* New York: John Wiley & Sons, Inc., 1958.

Leighton, A. H. *My Name is Legion: Foundations for a Theory of Man's Response to Culture.* New York: Basic Books. Inc.. 1959.

Blumenthal, R., & Meltzoff, J. *The Day Treatment Center: Principles, Application, and Evaluation.* Springfield, Illinois: Charles C. Thomas, 1966.

Kubie, Lawrence S. Pitfalls of Community Psychiatry. *Archives of General Psychiatry,* March 1968, 18, 257-266.

Redlich, F. C., & Pepper, Max. Are Social Psychiatry and Community Psychiatry Subspecialties of Psychiatry? *American Journal of Psychiatry,* October 1968, 124, 1343-1350.

Recommended by Camille Jeffers, M.S.W.

Three Generations: Case Material in Low Income Urban Living. Washington: Cross-Tell, 1966.
Living Poor. Ann Arbor, Michigan: Ann Arbor Publishers, 1967.

Recommended by Leo Srole, Ph.D.

————, et al. *Mental Health in the Metropolis: The Midtown Manhattan Study.* New York: McGraw-Hill Book Co., 1962.
Poverty and Mental Health: Conceptual and Taxonomic Problems. *Poverty and Mental Health,* Psychiatric Research Report No. 21, M. Greenblatt, P. E. Emery, & B. C. Glueck, Jr. (Eds.). Washington: American Psychiatric Association, 1967.

Recommended by several faculty

Riese, Hertha. *Heal the Hurt Child.* Chicago: University of Chicago Press, 1962.
Pearl, Arthur, & Riessman, F. *New Careers for the Poor.* New York: Free Press, 1965.
Chilman, C. S. *Growing Up Poor.* Washington: U.S. Department of Health, Education, and Welfare, SRS No. 109, June 1969.
Group for the Advancement of Psychiatry, Committee on Medical Education. *Education for Community Psychiatry,* Report No. 64. New York: March 1967.

APPENDIX C

PRE-INSTITUTE QUESTIONNAIRE

June 6, 1968

To Members of the Institute:

I would greatly appreciate your help in the task of following the flow of ideas in the forthcoming Institute for Training in Community and Social Psychiatry.

It will be my responsibility, as a consulting sociologist, to observe, to interpret, and to report back to you what happens at this meeting. For this purpose, the enclosed questionnaire has been selected for you to complete *prior* to the opening of the institute.

Your answers will be kept in strictest confidence. The information will be tabulated by me and made available only in the form of summaries and reports.

Please sign your name in the space provided on the enclosed envelope. This signature is required to allow for the follow-up study which I hope will make this a more meaningful study than is possible with an anonymous survey.

I would like to thank you for your cooperation, the request that, after placing the completed questionnaire in the enclosed envelope, you return it to me on Sunday evening, June 9.

Sincerely yours,

Samuel W. Bloom, Ph.D.
Professor of Sociology

BAKER-SCHULBERG CMHI SCALE

Instruction. Please read each of the statements carefully, in the order in which it appears, and for each one indicate to what extent you personally agree or disagree with it. You should do this by circling next to each statement the *one of* the six symbols which best represents your own feeling about the statement.

Circle AAA, if you *strongly agree*
Circle AA, if you *moderately agree*
Circle A, if you *slightly agree*

Circle DDD, if you *strongly disagree*
Circle DD, if you *moderately disagree*
Circle D, if you *slightly disagree*

	Strongly agree	Moderately agree	Slightly agree	Slightly disagree	Moderately disagree	Strongly disagree
1. Every mental health center should have formally associated with it a local citizen's board assigned significant responsibilities.	AAA	AA	A	D	DD	DDD
2. Our time-tested pattern of diagnosing and treating individual patients is still the optimal way for us to function professionally.	AAA	AA	A	D	DD	DDD

	Strongly agree	Moderately agree	Slightly agree	Slightly disagree	Moderately disagree	Strongly disagree
3. With our limited professional resources it makes more sense to use established knowledge to treat the mentally ill rather than trying to deal with the social conditions which may cause mental illness.	AAA	AA	A	D	DD	DDD
4. Our responsibility for patients extends beyond the contact we have with them in the mental health center.	AAA	AA	A	D	DD	DDD
5. A significant part of the psychiatrist's job consists of finding out who the mentally disordered are and where they are located in the community.	AAA	AA	A	D	DD	DDD
6. Such public health programs as primary preventive services are still of little value to the mental health field.	AAA	AA	A	D	DD	DDD
7. A mental health program should direct particular attention to groups of people who are potentially vulnerable to upsetting pressures.	AAA	AA	A	D	DD	DDD
8. The planning and operation of mental health programs are professional functions which should not be influenced by citizen pressures.	AAA	AA	A	D	DD	DDD

9. Mental health programs should give a high priority to lowering the rate of new cases in a community by reducing harmful environmental conditions. AAA AA A D DD DDD

10. The mental health specialist should seek to extend his effectiveness by working through other people. AAA AA A D DD DDD

11. A mental health professional can only be responsible for the mentally ill who come to him; he cannot be responsible for those who do not seek him out. AAA AA A D DD DDD

12. Our program emphasis should be shifted from the clinical model, directed at specific patients, to the public health model, focusing upon populations. AAA AA A D DD DDD

13. Understanding of the community in which we work should be made a central focus in the training of mental health professionals. AAA AA A D DD DDD

14. The control of mental illness is a goal that can only be attained through psychiatric treatment. AAA AA A D DD DDD

15. A mental health professional assumes responsibility not only for his current caseload but also for unidentified potentially maladjusted people in the community. AAA AA A D DD DDD

16. Our current emphasis upon the problems of individual patients is a relatively ineffective approach for easing a community's total psychiatric problem. AAA AA A D DD DDD

	Strongly agree	Moderately agree	Slightly agree	Slightly disagree	Moderately disagree	Strongly disagree
17. Our professional mandate is to treat individual patients and not the harmful influences in society.	AAA	AA	A	D	DD	DDD
18. Our efforts to involve citizens in mental health programs have not produced sufficient payoff to make it worth our while.	AAA	AA	A	D	DD	DDD
19. The locus of mental illness must be viewed as extending beyond the individual, and into the family, the community, and the society.	AAA	AA	A	D	DD	DDD
20. Mental health professionals can be concerned for their patient's welfare only when having them in active treatment.	AAA	AA	A	D	DD	DDD
21. Mental health consultation is a necessary service which we must provide to community care-givers who can help in the care of the mentally ill.	AAA	AA	A	D	DD	DDD
22. Caregiving agents who worked with the patient before and during his contact at the mental health center should be included in the formulation of treatment plans.	AAA	AA	A	D	DD	DDD
23. A psychiatrist can only provide useful services to those people with whom he has direct personal contact.	AAA	AA	A	D	DD	DDD

24. Skill in collaborating with nonmental health professionals is relatively unimportant to the success of our work with the mentally ill.

AAA   AA   A   D   DD   DDD

25. The mental health center is only one part of a comprehensive community mental health program.

AAA   AA   A   D   DD   DDD

26. Mental health professionals should only provide their services to individuals whom society defines as mentally ill or who voluntarily seek these services.

AAA   AA   A   D   DD   DDD

27. We should deal with people who are not yet sick by helping them to develop ways for coping with expected life difficulties.

AAA   AA   A   D   DD   DDD

28. We should not legitimately be concerned with modifying aspects of our patient's environment but rather in bolstering his ability to cope with it.

AAA   AA   A   D   DD   DDD

29. It is a poor treatment policy to allow non-psychiatrists to perform traditional psychiatric functions.

AAA   AA   A   D   DD   DDD

30. Since we do not know enough about prevention, mental health programs should direct their prime efforts toward treating the mentally ill rather than developing prevention programs.

AAA   AA   A   D   DD   DDD

31. The hospital and community should strive for the goal of each participating in the affairs and activities of the other.

AAA   AA   A   D   DD   DDD

32. Social action is required to insure the success of mental health programs.

AAA   AA   A   D   DD   DDD

	Strongly agree	Moderately agree	Slightly agree	Slightly disagree	Moderately disagree	Strongly disagree
33. In view of the professional manpower shortage, existing resources should be used for treatment programs rather than prevention programs.	AAA	AA	A	D	DD	DDD
34. Each mental health center should join the health and welfare counsel of each community it serves.	AAA	AA	A	D	DD	DDD
35. The responsible mental health professional should become an agent for social change.	AAA	AA	A	D	DD	DDD
36. We can make more effective use of our skills by intensively treating a limited number of patients instead of working indirectly with many patients.	AAA	AA	A	D	DD	DDD
37. By and large, the practice of good psychiatry does not require very much knowledge about sociology and anthropology.	AAA	AA	A	D	DD	DDD
38. Community agencies working with the patient should not be involved with the different phases of a patient's hospitalization.	AAA	AA	A	D	DD	DDD

BACKGROUND DATA SHEET

TO HELP UNDERSTAND THE RELATIONSHIP BETWEEN OPINIONS ABOUT MENTAL HEALTH ISSUES AND ONE'S PROFESSIONAL BACKGROUND, WE ARE SEEKING BRIEF DATA ABOUT YOUR EXPERIENCES AND INTERESTS. PLEASE PROVIDE THE APPROPRIATE RESPONSES TO THE FOLLOWING QUESTIONS.

1. What is your sex?   Male _____   Female _____

2. How old are you at present?   Below 30 _____
                                        30-40 _____
                                        40-50 _____
                                        Above 50 _____

3. What academic or professional degrees have you received (e.g., M.D., Ph.D., M.S.W., B.S., etc.)? _____

4. In what year did you receive your highest academic or professional degree? _____

5. After completing your basic course of professional training have you obtained further systematic training in any of the following areas? Check the appropriate ones.

   Community mental health techniques _____   Social Psychiatry _____
   Psychotherapy or psychoanalysis _____   Somatic approaches _____
   Research _____   (Other (_____))

6. Approximately what percentage of your professional work week do you spend in each of the following activities?

Administration _____
Consulting with community agencies _____
Research _____
Supervising others in my facility _____
Teaching _____
Treating patients _____
Other (_____) _____

100%

7. To which professional organizations do you belong? Check those of which you are a member.

American Group Psychotherapy Association _____
American Nursing Association _____
American Occupational Therapy Association _____
American Orthopsychiatric Association _____
American Psychiatric Association _____
American Psychoanalytic Association (or local society) _____
American Psychological Association (list Divisions:_____) _____
Group for Advancement of Psychiatry _____
National League for Nursing _____
Society for Biological Psychiatry _____
Other (Specify) _____ _____

8. Check those of the following areas in which you feel a strong enough interest to keep up with new developments.

Biochemistry _____   Individual psychotherapy _____
Community Mental Health _____   Milieu therapy _____
Culture and personality _____   Neurology _____
Epidemiology _____   Neuropharmacology _____
Genetics _____   Social Psychiatry _____
Group psychotherapy _____   Other (_____)

9. If simultaneous symposia were being held on each of the following topics, which would you attend? Rank your first preference "1," second "2," third "3," and last "4."

Recent advanced in Community Mental Health _____
Recent advances in Milieu Therapy _____
Recent advances in Psychotherapy _____
Recent advances in Somatic Therapy _____

10. Indicate by circling the appropriate number how strongly you identify with *each* of the following orientations:

	Very Strongly		*Average*		*Not at All*
Somatic (organic)	1	2	3	4	5
Psychotherapeutic	1	2	3	4	5
Sociotherapeutic (milieu)	1	2	3	4	5
Community Mental Health	1	2	3	4	5

11. In which *one* of the following settings do you spend the majority of your professional work week?

University or Medical School ———
Mental Hospital ———
General Hospital ———
Community Clinic ———

Private Practice ———
School System ———
Industry ———
Other (———)

SEMANTIC DIFFERENTIAL SCALE

Instructions: The purpose of this questionnaire is to measure the meanings of COMMUNITY MENTAL HEALTH to various people by having them judge it against a series of descriptive scales. In taking this test, please make your judgments on the basis of what it means to *you.* You are to rate the concept on each of these scales in order.

Here is how you are to use these scales:

If you feel that COMMUNITY MENTAL HEALTH is *very closely related* to one end of the scale, you should place your check mark as follows:

valuable __X_:___:___:___:___:___:___: worthless

or

valuable ___:___:___:___:___:___: X_: worthless

If you feel that COMMUNITY MENTAL HEALTH is *quite closely related* to one or the other end of the scale (but not extremely), you should place your check mark as follows:

valuable ___: X_:___:___:___:___: worthless

or

valuable ___:___:___:___:___: X_:___: worthless

If the concept seems only slightly related to one side as opposed to the other side (but is not really neutral), then you should check as follows:

valuable ___:___: X_:___:___:___: worthless

or

valuable ___:___:___:___: X_:___:___: worthless

The direction toward which you check, of course, depends upon which of the two ends of the scale seem most characteristic of COMMUNITY MENTAL HEALTH.

If you consider the concept to be *neutral* on the scale, both sides of the scale *equally associated* with the concept, or if the scale is *completely irrelevant,* unrelated to the concept, then you should place your check mark in the middle space:

valuable ___:___:___: X_:___:___:___: worthless

IMPORTANT:
  (1) Place your check marks in the middle of the spaces, not on the boundaries:

  X
____:____:___ X _:____:____:___:
  this not
  this

  (2) Be sure you check every scale—*do not omit any*
  (3) Never put more than one check mark on a single scale.

Work at a fairly high speed through this task. Do not worry or puzzle over individual items. It is your first impressions, the immediate "feelings" about the items, that we want. On the other hand, please do not be careless, because we want your true impressions.

COMMUNITY MENTAL HEALTH

good	:	:	:	:	:	:	bad
ineffective	:	:	:	:	:	:	effective
irrelevant	:	:	:	:	:	:	relevant
timely	:	:	:	:	:	:	untimely
new	:	:	:	:	:	:	old hat
regressive	:	:	:	:	:	:	progressive
wise	:	:	:	:	:	:	foolish
simple	:	:	:	:	:	:	complex
wrong	:	:	:	:	:	:	right
sophisticated	:	:	:	:	:	:	naive
narrow	:	:	:	:	:	:	broad
rash	:	:	:	:	:	:	considered
realistic	:	:	:	:	:	:	unrealistic
needed	:	:	:	:	:	:	unneeded
unimportant	:	:	:	:	:	:	important
strong	:	:	:	:	:	:	weak
sterile	:	:	:	:	:	:	productive
conflicting	:	:	:	:	:	:	cooperative
active	:	:	:	:	:	:	passive

Post-Institute Questionnaire

To Institute Participants:

As part of the effort to understand and learn from this institute, the enclosed questionnaire includes several types of inquiry:

(1) An assessment of the group experience in your discussion group
(2) Open questions to elicit your general reactions to the institute itself
(3) Attitude questions that repeat the preliminary questionnaire sent to you before the institute

I would like to repeat my assurance that all individual responses will be treated with the strictest confidence. To study change, and to allow the important option of follow-up interview, some method of identifying each response is necessary. For this purpose, I am asking you to sign your name at the bottom of this sheet. Immediately upon receipt, the questionnaire is given a code number, and the name removed. No one but myself will have access to the code, and no individual response will be identifiable in my reports.

Early in the fall of 1968, I will send to you a written report summarizing the institute evaluation, and soon thereafter, you will have the opportunity to meet again as a group to discuss the findings and my interpretation. Your participation, of course, is entirely voluntary.

May I urge that you complete the enclosed materials by June 16, 1968 and return them to me in the enclosed envelope.

Sincerely yours,

Samuel W. Bloom, Ph.D.
Professor of Sociology

_____

(Please print name here)

Group Rating Scale

Purpose: The purpose of this rating sheet is to measure your perception, *as a group member,* of how your workshop group functioned.

Please rate the *actual* behavior that was expressed in the group by drawing a circle around the number that seems to be the position of the group.

INSTRUCTIONS

Notice that the scale has statement "A" on the left and statement "B" on the right. You are to select numbers 1 to 7 according to your agreement with the statements as follows:

7—Practically all statement A, not statement B

6—Very strongly statement A, very weakly statement B

5—Slightly more statement A than statement B

3—Slightly more statement B than statement A

2—Very strongly statement B and very weakly statement A

1—Practically all statement B and not statement A

STATEMENT "A"							STATEMENT "B"
1. Worked intensely	7	6	5	3	2	1	Worked relaxed
2. Held a high standard	7	6	5	3	2	1	Compromised
3. Dominant leadership	7	6	5	3	2	1	Without leadership
4. High commitment to problem	7	6	5	3	2	1	No personal commitment
5. High production of ideas	7	6	5	3	2	1	Low production of ideas
6. Worked at fast pace	7	6	5	3	2	1	Got bogged down
7. Was physically restless	7	6	5	3	2	1	Sat motionless
8. Members tended to seek personal recognition	7	6	5	3	2	1	Members sought understanding of others' ideas
9. Cordial exchange of ideas	7	6	5	3	2	1	Impersonal exchange of ideas
10. Concern for group unity	7	6	5	3	2	1	Not concerned with group unity
11. Warm and intimate	7	6	5	3	2	1	Formal and objective
12. Emphasis on theory	7	6	5	3	2	1	Emphasis on concrete
13. High concern for details	7	6	5	3	2	1	Low concern for details
14. Organized and on course	7	6	5	3	2	1	Discussion wandered
15. New ideas encouraged	7	6	5	3	2	1	New ideas resisted
16. Discussion easygoing and calm	7	6	5	3	2	1	Discussion emotional
17. Open conflict	7	6	5	3	2	1	Conflict ignored
18. Deference shown	7	6	5	3	2	1	No special treatment given
19. High concern for rules	7	6	5	3	2	1	Discussion free and spontaneous
20. Discussion was intelligent	7	6	5	3	2	1	Discussion was dull
21. Over-all rating excellent	7	6	5	3	2	1	Unsatisfactory

REACTION TO INSTITUTE QUESTIONNAIRE

This section is designed to give you the opportunity to react to the institute itself. (Please write on the back of each page, if necessary.)

1. Did this institute add to your personal understanding of community mental health? If it did, what kinds of information and understanding were most meaningful to you?

2. (a) What central questions or issues concerning community mental health are, in your view, the most critical?

   (b) Were all these issues discussed in the institute? If not, which ones were either missed or inadequately treated?

   (c) If important issues were not treated, why not?

3. Where do you think you stand in your attitudes toward community mental health *compared with* the general climate of opinion of the Boston University Division of Psychiatry? Have your attitudes been affected by this institute?

   If so, how?

4. As freely as possible, and from your own personal view, would you comment on the format of the institute. What, if any, aspects were highlights? Were there unexpected events, content, or problems? What, if anything, would you have liked to see done differently?

After years of dedicated farming and toil, she now believed there was more to life than material success. She believed in Santa, in Christmas and, most importantly, she believed she was still a kid at heart.

The farm looked fresh and beautiful through her renewed sight. A joy in her heart burst out into song.

"It's the most wonderful time of the year…" she sang as she skipped over the field toward the flickering light coming from her farmhouse.

"Thank you!" Tiberius shouted as he ran back toward the stables.

Ziggy already had the reindeer hitched up and ready to go. Ben had a cartload of small containers he began loading into the sack. Tomo threw some lines and climbing gear into the sleigh. Ziggy hopped up and was ready to go.

"Hold it," Tiberius commanded. "Tomo is going with you."

"What?" Tomo and Ziggy asked at the same time.

"You read the letter," Tiberius lectured. "There is a steep canyon and they need climbing gear. Those are two things Tomo will be able to help with."

Tomo jumped in the sleigh and they were out of sight in a flash, leaving behind a swirl of snow.

The storm over Brooks Range had turned into a blinding blizzard. Snow swirled in all directions. The wind was howling over the high ridges. The sleigh circled around the area but Ziggy and Tomo could not see a canyon. Despite Rudolph's nose burning as brightly as ever; it was not enough to find the lost explorers.

"Ziggy, please land the sleigh," Tomo requested. "We need to find the canyon. If we find the edge, we can walk around it until we find Jasper and Mithra."

Ziggy carefully landed the sleigh. Tomo put on her climbing harness and tethered herself to the front of the reindeer team. She told Ziggy and the reindeer to stay far behind her. Without a trace of fear, she blindly marched forward.

Just like her experience on Mount Everest, each step was a step into the unknown. After a few minutes, she took a step forward but her foot kept going down. The reindeer felt a sudden tug on the tether. They stopped.

"Found it," Tomo called, dangling over the canyon wall. Before the reindeer had a chance to pull her up, she had already climbed to them.

Tomo led Rudolph and the rest of the team around the edge of the canyon. Now that they knew where the edge was, they just had to circle it and find the group.

After a few minutes of walking they heard a cry over the howling of the wind.

"Over here," Jasper yelled. "We're over here."

Ziggy and Tomo were surprised to find not two, but three people with Jasper.

"What are you doing here?" Ziggy shouted over the storm.

"We think we may have found where I came from," Jasper replied. "We need to get to the bottom of the canyon and collect any cosmic dust that's down there."

Before anyone could say another word, Tomo, still in her climbing harness, flung Santa's sack on her back and headed straight for the edge.

"Take this," Mrs. Bentley yelled as she handed her instrument to Tomo. "This will point you to each speck of cosmic dust."

Tomo took the sensor and disappeared over the edge of the canyon.

"Who was that?" Jasper asked.

"Tomo," Ziggy answered. "She joined us yesterday. She's a world champion climber. If you need something down there, she'll get it."

Tomo dropped down into the abyss with only a headlamp to guide her. The sides of the canyon were slippery, but she had no problem making a quick descent. When she hit the bottom, it felt like landing on an ocean of snow. Waves of snow moved her up and down.

She looked at the sensor and it pointed to the center of a wave. She scooped the snow into a container and held the sensor up to it. It was still reading the cosmic dust signature.

"Got one," she said aloud.

She continued to scoop snow from the center of each wave until she had collected about fifty containers. The

snowfield was calm, indicating that all the core retrieved. She was surprised to fling the full s shoulders and find it was still as light as a fe scrambled up the wall with incredible speed.

She arrived at the top to find everyone equipment packed away in the sleigh. She hopped i sack and the sleigh launched into the blizzard.

"Did you find anything?" Jasper asked nervously.

"I found about fifty samples."

Jasper's face began to melt with tears of joy. Mithr over and smooshed the drops back into his face. Jasper, her own tears were doing no damage.

After a short time, the sleigh landed on a snow-c field. The sky was still overcast, but there was no blizz

"Where are we?" Jasper asked.

"We're back on my farm," Mithra responded s looking around at her surroundings.

It was night at the farm and the sleigh landed far fror house.

"Mrs. Bentley, this is your stop," Ziggy said.

Mithra and her mother looked at each other.

"I want to go with you," Mrs. Bentley said.

"Santa Claus is about children," Ziggy tried to explain. " still need Mithra's help but I can't take you with us."

Mithra turned to her mother and said, "Thank you Mo Thank you for always being there to help me. I need to do tl on my own now."

Mrs. Bentley stepped out of the sleigh. Tears streame down her face. All the emotions from the past forty-eigh hours flooded her heart. She had actually found the quiverin snow that had captivated her imagination since her youth Her daughter was now an independent young woman sharing her passion for knowledge. Life was more than what could be observed with instruments. She believed again.

PART TWO

14

The morning of December 5th saw the entire Naughty Team gathered together for the very first time. They were assembled in Santa's office, excited to start their preparations for Operation Naughty Redemption. Mrs. Claus, Ziggy, and Scout were seated at the table with the kids. Jasper was outside, eagerly awaiting the creation of additional snowmen.

Mithra and Nebo were brought up to speed on the purpose of the team. Tiberius explained the significance of the Naughty List and the events that had brought them all together. He studied each face in the room and, with the exception of Nebo, quickly assessed the role they would play in the plan for rescuing Santa.

"Mithra Bentley is our weather expert. She'll read the snowflakes, search for clues in regard to weather patterns and put the elements of our unique environment to work for our advantage. Her first task is to build snowmen using the snow taken from the canyon yesterday. Then she'll figure out the best route to get us to Baekdu Island.

"Ben David is our military planner. Ben will organize our training and develop the logistics of the rescue.

"Gus Rauch is our communications expert. He will use his ability to understand the language of animals in order to give us valuable insight to the many types of creatures we're sure to encounter both here and in the surroundings of Baekdu Island.

"Tomo Gozen is a world champion athlete. Her specialty is climbing. She will work with Ben to help us scale Baekdu Island. Her skills have already proven to be very useful in recovering the cosmic dust samples.

"Josef Ruprecht is a computer genius. He has already begun working on a way to gain entry inside the Eastern Industries network. We hope he'll be able to access the plans for the factory on Baekdu Island and find a weak point for entry. Once underway, Josef will help us neutralize the surveillance network Eastern Industries has in place around the island.

"Nebo, I'm not sure how you will fit into our team. Would you mind explaining why you took the journey up here?"

Nebo looked around the room. He displayed the same passive look that Mithra had grown accustomed to. He stood up to address the group. Nebo was taller than the other kids and his complexion was darker. He carried himself more like an old man than a child. Only his youthful face indicated his age.

"I am here to save Marduk," Nebo began. "I believe Santa Claus is the most recent resurrection of Marduk. The people that took him are the agents of chaos and I have come to defeat them."

"Wow!" Gus erupted with anger. "Santa is Marduk? What are you saying? I've never even heard of a Marduk! I think you need to go back home, Nebo. You don't know what you're talking about and you obviously don't understand Christmas."

Nebo nodded and turned toward the door.

"Wait!" Tiberius said. "Let us hear him out. It's the least we can do considering the long journey he undertook to get here."

"Please explain more about Marduk," Mrs. Claus said warmly. "I think the children would be very interested in your background."

Nebo still showed no emotion. He refused to get riled up over any conversation. He turned back toward the table.

"I come from Hillah, Iraq," Nebo began. "Hillah is located over the ruins of the ancient city of Babylon. As early as four thousand years ago, my people celebrated a holiday called Zagmuk. Zagmuk was the time of year when chaos would try to take over the world. Everything was at risk.

"Marduk was the patron deity of Babylon and, as such, held the highest position in the Babylonian pantheon. He was the king of gods. At the end of each year, Tiamat, the god of chaos, would confine Marduk inside a mountain. The Babylonians would worry that Marduk would not return and chaos would rule. For them, chaos would signal the end of the world. The separation between the earth and the sea would end. All would be lost.

"Even our King would lose his power during this time. It was a time of decay across the land. The sun was marching to the south and no one knew if it would ever return."

Mrs. Claus smiled. She knew the story well, but had not heard it for many years. The elves and kids in the room listened attentively. Even Gus had lost some of his anger as Nebo continued his story.

"For the people of Babylon, this was a tense time. They performed ceremonies to cleanse their sins. The ceremonies focused on the rebirth of people and nature itself. Even the king participated in these ceremonies. He regained his authority over the people only after his own cleansing.

"As part of the ritual, a statue representing Marduk's son, Nabu, would arrive at the city gates in a barge along with more barges carrying the statues of other gods. The gods would join together before beginning their journey to recover Marduk.

"Nabu would lead a procession of the gods to the mountain where Marduk was confined. An epic fight would take place and, at the end, only a door would stand between them and Marduk. Nabu would pound down the door with his fists and Marduk would be freed.

"The power of all the gods would be placed into Marduk, so he could prevail over chaos. The people's destiny would be chosen and soon life would return to normal. Crops would be sowed, trading would resume, and, most importantly, the sun would begin its journey back to the top of the sky."

Everyone in the room was captivated. They now had an understanding of what Nebo was saying. Santa was the one trapped in the mountain. In Nebo's eyes, the Naughty Team would be the group to free him.

"Are you saying that you're a god?" Gus asked Nebo sarcastically.

"I am not a god," Nebo answered. "In my religion, the gods represent aspects of nature. They serve a purpose of educating people about the natural cycle of the world. In essence, Zagmuk was a twelve-day celebration of nature's renewal."

"Twelve days? God's son? Peace, cleansing of sins, and feasting?" Gus asked ready to give his own answer. "Sounds a lot like Christmas."

"Exactly," Nebo responded. "Zagmuk was Christmas before there was a Christmas. I am here to help save Christmas, just like all of you. Zagmuk is all but lost to the ages, but it continues to live on in the observance of Christmas."

Gus was still not convinced Nebo shared their common goal. He interpreted Nebo's winter celebration as just another attack on the traditions of Christmas.

"How exactly did Zagmuk become Christmas?" Gus pressed Nebo. Gus was obviously irritated and could not put the whole thing together.

"It did not," Mrs. Claus replied.

She walked over to Gus and put her hand on his shoulder. The warmth and friendship that always shone in her face radiated down through her hand into Gus. He immediately relaxed and the anger left him as quickly as it had boiled up.

"Christmas is the winter celebration of our time. But people have been celebrating a winter holiday long before Zagmuk. Since man first walked the earth, winter has been a time of observing decay and embracing renewal. Villages became quiet as fields went barren. Animals that had been raised during the warmer months were slaughtered since there were no means to feed them throughout the winter. With all that meat available and no way to store it for very long, communities created holidays that included feasts and other relevant customs. The further north one goes, the greater the impact of the change of seasons, and rituals adapt accordingly.

"In our present time, we know the sun will return each year based on astronomical calendars and research. Our ancestors did not know that. They feared the sun's departure and were relieved when the days got longer again.

"The Romans celebrated Saturnalia. To the north of them, people celebrated the great Yule Feast. Many of our Christmas customs come from these two midwinter festivals.

"Gus, you celebrate Christmas in a very spiritual way that connects you to your religion. I think you have a beautiful way of celebrating. But please do not expect everyone to think of Christmas the same way you do. One of the best things about Christmas is the way people observe it according to their own customs and beliefs."

Mrs. Claus took her hand off Gus's shoulder and returned to her seat. He was no longer angry, but he was still not happy with the way the discussion had turned.

"We need to put Christ back in Christmas," Gus demanded.

"We need to put Marduk back in Zagmuk," Nebo countered.

Gus's face turned red with anger again. He stood up and asked, "How can we save Christmas if no one knows what Christmas is?"

"Fried chicken," Tomo offered.

Everyone except Gus chuckled at Tomo's odd comment. Soon the chuckling grew to laughter. Eventually Gus smiled at the deadpan line from Tomo.

Tomo had everyone's attention.

"Fried chicken is what Christmas is to my family," Tomo continued. "Every year on Christmas Eve, we go to the local fried chicken restaurant and wait for hours to pick up our meal. Some of my most precious Christmas memories are from that time, standing in line.

"My parents have always been very strict with me. I am only allowed to eat food that will advance my training. We are a very serious family and conversations only consist of serious matters.

"But when we get on that silly line on Christmas Eve, my father lets go of his stern manner, loosens up and tells jokes to my sister, Kiso, and me. We laugh the whole time. It's the only occasion when I see my father grin with delight. I enjoy it so much I never want us to reach the front of the line.

"When we get home, we sit down to the meal and my mother tells us stories about Santa Claus. I will always treasure the look of wonder in Kiso's eyes as she cherishes every detail. We end the night playing games before heading to bed.

"Then my father reads to us while we're nestled under our covers:

> *'Twas the night before Christmas, when all through the house*
> *Not a creature was stirring, not even a mouse.*
> *The stockings were hung by the chimney with care,*
> *In hopes that St. Nicholas soon would be there.*

"Kiso is so excited that she spends most of the night talking about Santa and the wonderful day our family has shared. It's the closest I feel to my family all year long.

"My Christmas is different than yours, but I like my family's tradition as much as you like yours. I want your Christmas to be right for you," Tomo said directly to Gus. "No matter how any of us celebrate Christmas, I think we all want it to continue to be ours, not the uniform Winterval celebration that Eastern Industries is trying to force upon the world."

Everyone in the room sat in silence for a moment and appreciated the brief glimpse of Tomo's inner self. Underneath her carefully practiced, austere façade, they could see a little girl. They saw she was swept away with emotion from within, but her practice and training would not let it surface completely. The struggle inside her was apparent.

Tiberius was especially moved. He could appreciate the trouble Tomo had with her stern parents. Tiberius had little family life. He pitied himself for not even having an experience as simple as a long wait in line to connect with his family. His father never told him a joke. His mother never told a story. He envied Tomo's memories of Christmas.

Gus gazed at Tomo as he stood up. She was looking down at the floor now. He appreciated the great effort that went into her explanation. He saw the determination still evident in Nebo's erect posture. He noticed the elves plaintive stares back at him.

"I guess Christmas is many things to many people," Gus said contritely. "I'm sure we all honor it in a different way. For me, it's about communing with God's creatures. For Tomo, it's spending rare quality time with family. For Nebo, it's the victory of order over chaos.

"I'm sorry, I thought my way was the only way to keep Christmas. Thanks for sharing your story, Tomo. I will work with Nebo to get Santa back," Gus said with conviction. "I will do whatever I can to save Christmas for all of us."

Tiberius was the only person in the room that did not really understand what all the Christmas fuss was about. He had agreed to lead this mission because he finally felt he was being appreciated. He liked the group around him, but Christmas was an afterthought. He was eager to change the subject.

"Alrighty then. Nebo, welcome to the team. Now let's get back to planning," Tiberius said. The rest of the group was shocked by his abruptness.

"Ben please share your training schedule with the group."

Ben presented the following schedule:

Operation Naughty Redemption Training Schedule
> *6 AM: Stretching and Exercise*
> *7 AM: Breakfast*
> *8 AM: Specialized Training with Tomo and Ben*
> *9 AM: Morning Debriefing*
> *10 AM: Individual Tasks*
> *Noon: Lunch*
> *1 PM: Individual Tasks*
> *6 PM: Dinner*
> *7 PM: Relaxation and Games*
> *9 PM: Sleep*

It was almost 10 o'clock in the morning. Tiberius wanted to implement the schedule right away, so he wasted no time in giving everyone their assignment.

"Gus, please work with the animals and see if we can get some information about Baekdu Island from the birds that have flown over. Mithra and Tomo, please work with the elves to build Jasper some additional snowmen. Ben, please see if you can figure out some type of transportation to Baekdu Island. I'll stay here with Nebo and determine how he may be able to help."

After most of the room had cleared out, Tiberius turned to Nebo. "Please tell me more about Zagmuk and the mountain. We may be able to learn something from those past battles."

"Please do," Mrs. Claus added. "I would love to hear more. It has been a long time since someone has talked about Marduk up here."

"You've heard this story before?" Tiberius asked.

"Yes I have," Mrs. Claus said. "And I always thought that eventually we'd have a visitor from Hillah."

15

Outside, in the North Pole village, Mithra found Jasper anxiously waiting for her.

"Are you ready to build some snowmen?" he pleaded.

"That's what we're here for," she replied gesturing toward Tomo.

Mithra got the containers with the snow they had collected from the canyon and opened the first one. She tried to give it to Jasper, but he backed away, waving his hands.

"Oh no," he said shaking his head. "I can't build the snowmen. If our cores get bonded by the snow, we'll become a quivering pile."

Mithra understood and passed a jar to Tomo. Tomo dumped the snow onto the ground and started building. Mithra grabbed a jar for herself and worked next to her. It took a few minutes to roll the first snowballs.

"This is going to take a long time," Mithra observed.

The two girls grinned at each other. They faced a large task, but it was especially gratifying to know that the completed snowmen would be alive.

After a short time, their activity caught the attention of an elf who was walking by. An elf can never pass up the opportunity to build a snowman. Before long, many elves were assisting in the project and rolling snowballs all over the place. Some ran into the workshops to fetch coal, buttons, carrots, and pipes to help spruce them up.

"No pipes!" Jasper ordered. "Those won't be necessary."

Mithra laughed at Jasper, recalling their first meeting.

Within an hour, fifty snowmen stood in place on the outskirts of the village. There was just one problem; not one of the snowmen showed any sign of movement.

"Is this normal?" Mithra asked Jasper. "Shouldn't they be mobile by now?"

"How would I know?" Jasper replied. "Do you remember anything about your own birth?"

Everyone was confounded. The elves murmured to each other. All they could come up with was that the core snowflake must be in the wrong spot.

Mithra ran back to the workshop and grabbed her mother's cosmic dust sensor. She scanned a snowman and found the cosmic signature in the head. She scanned a few more and they also seemed to be built correctly.

"I need to look at the core snowflake under a microscope," Mithra said turning to Tomo. "Please use this sensor and see if you can isolate it. I'm going to get my photography equipment. I should be able to see if the snowflake looks identical to Jasper's core snowflake. I still have a picture of that."

Tomo slowly picked apart one of the snowballs, using the sensor to track the core. She was down to just a few snowflakes when Mithra returned with her photography equipment. Tomo loaded a slide with the core snowflake and Mithra inspected it carefully. She noticed the snowflake was not formed properly. It had been melted and refrozen.

"As I suspected — this is not a snowflake," Mithra said to Tomo, "This is more like sleet. Jasper's core was found at the center of a perfect, dendrite snowflake."

"What type of snowflake?" Tomo asked.

"A dendrite snowflake has six arms coming out of the center," Mithra explained. "It would be the type of snowflake that is often seen in pictures and paper cutouts.

"These types of snowflakes are formed around 5 degrees Fahrenheit. There must be something about that shape that allows the cosmic dust to come alive."

"Can a reindeer take it up to the sky, like Donner did with Jasper?" Tomo asked pointing up to the snowing clouds.

"I don't think so," Mithra replied with a pensive look. "Jasper knew where to land. If we drop this dust particle into the sky, it should form a nice snowflake, but we won't know when or where it would land. What we need to do is create the snowflake in a controlled environment."

Tomo sat down in the snow and traced patterns with her finger. She did not know what to do next. Jasper was disappointed in their lack of progress. He walked around the different snowmen to see if any showed a sign of life.

"Let's take a break," Mithra suggested. "I have an idea, but we're going to need some equipment."

She turned toward the elves and said, "Thanks for all the help this morning. We're going to see if we can make a machine to create a dendrite snowflake and solve our problem."

Tomo and Mithra headed back inside for lunch. Most of the team had already started eating. Josef was the only kid missing.

"Where's Josef?" Mithra asked the group.

"He thinks he may have found a back door into the Eastern Industries network. He said he'll skip lunch since the vulnerability may not last very long," Tiberius answered.

Mithra then told the rest of the group about her failure to animate the snowmen. She explained that the cosmic dust was not attached to the right type of snowflake.

"I know how to make the perfect dendrite snowflake," Mithra added. "I've done this back on my farm in Jericho. I'll need some supplies to make the device."

"What do you need?" Ziggy asked. "Our elves can probably build something for you."

"I need an insulated cylinder about two feet high," Mithra explained. "The cylinder needs to be able to cool itself at the bottom and heat up at the top. It's called a vapor diffusion chamber.

"I also need a piece of tungsten. You can get that from any incandescent light bulb."

Ziggy thought about the request. It would be easy to get tungsten as they had tons of Christmas lights that used incandescent bulbs. The vapor diffusion chamber, on the other hand, would need a little more thought before they could work on it.

"We can make the insulated cylinder with materials from the workshop," Ziggy offered to the group. "Chilling the bottom will be more difficult."

"Do you have a CO_2 fire extinguisher?" Mithra asked.

"Yes," Ziggy responded. "We have many of those in the workshop."

"Great," Mithra continued with growing excitement. "We can use those extinguishers to make dry ice. That will cool the bottom enough to achieve the low temperature we need. Then we can heat the top by creating a closed circuit with a battery."

"I'm not following along," Tiberius chimed in. "How does a tube that's hot on top and cold on the bottom make a snowflake?"

Mithra had a big grin by now. She was sure she could make it work. She explained the process to the group.

"When water is added to the top of the chamber, water vapor will diffuse down and create supersaturated air. This is similar to what is going on in a cloud. If a speck of cosmic dust is suspended from a tungsten filament in the middle of the chamber, the water vapor will be cold enough to begin to form the snowflake around the speck of dust.

"If we can keep the temperature around five degrees near the dust particle, then a nice dendrite snowflake will form around it. A few minutes in the chamber should be enough to get a decent-sized snowflake."

Ziggy completely grasped the concept and rushed to the workshop to construct the vapor diffusion chamber. Before Mithra and Tomo had finished lunch, Ziggy had the chamber complete. They regrouped where all the snowmen stood silently.

"Finally!" Jasper exclaimed as everyone gathered. "Are you going to be able to make a nice snowflake with that contraption?"

"I think so," Mithra replied. "Let's give it a try."

Mithra got the particle Tomo had isolated and touched the tungsten filament to it. She put it inside the vapor diffusion chamber. Ziggy had already cooled the bottom and warmed the top. Mithra put some water in the top and they waited for the process to occur.

No one could see inside the chamber. The wait was especially difficult for Jasper. At long last, he was so close to being reunited with his own kind. He constantly asked if the process was complete.

"Is it done yet? How long will it take? Will they look just like me?"

To someone else, his inquiries might have been annoying, but Mithra understood. Jasper had been alone for a very long time.

While they waited for the process, she thought about how to better isolate the cosmic dust. If she could quickly find the dust particle after the snowflake melted, she would be able to rebuild the snowmen within minutes of melting.

After five minutes went by, Mithra opened the chamber. Everyone held their breath.

"We have a snowflake!" Mithra shouted with joy. "It's even bigger than I expected."

Mithra handed the tungsten filament to Tomo. Tomo blew the snowflake into the snow and promptly rolled another head for the snowman and plopped it on top. The elves that were in the area made sure the face had the proper eyes and nose.

For a moment, the snowman was frozen still just like the others. Then it suddenly came to life. The arms formed and moved. The legs took on a more humanlike shape. Finally, the mouth opened. Everyone cheered.

"Hello Universe!" the snowman burst out.

Before he could stop himself, Jasper instinctively hugged the snowman. Mithra gasped, but nothing happened. He did not become entangled with the snowman and reduced to a pile of quivering snow. Apparently, two properly formed snowmen could interact without fear of conflicting signals.

"Hello friend," Jasper said as he stepped back from his new peer. "What's your name?"

"I don't know," the snowman replied, scratching his head. "I know I'm here, but I don't know who I am or where here is."

"You're in the North Pole," Jasper said, not realizing he was once new to this strange world. "What should we call you?"

"Slow down, Jasper," Tomo suggested. "Give him a little time to get used to his surroundings... And his new form."

A crowd of elves gathered around the new snowman. No one noticed Mithra working on the next one.

Mithra had taken the head of another snowman and smashed it on the ground. The scene would be a bit appalling to anyone else, but to Mithra it was routine. Her scientific mind only saw the snowman for what it currently was: a shaped pile of snow. No different than a pile of snowballs ready to be launched.

She attached a tungsten filament to her mother's cosmic dust sensor and dragged the filament through the flattened pile. After getting a positive reading, she pulled the filament back out and held the end of it under her microscopic photography equipment.

"Found it!" she excitedly yelled. "We should be able to have the rest of these snowmen all fixed up by dinner."

Mithra had been able to attach just the cosmic dust core to the filament with the help of her mother's sensor. She added some water to the vapor diffusion chamber and another snowflake was born.

"Here you go," she said looking at Tomo. "Another snowflake ready to be added to a snowman."

For the rest of the afternoon, Mithra, Tomo, and the elves put the snowmen back together with the improved snowflakes in their head. Each time a snowman came to life he shouted the greeting, "Hello Universe!"

"We are at the North Pole," the first snowman said to a group of others.

"What is the North Pole?" another asked.

"North of what?"

"What's your name?"

"I don't know, what's yours?"

"Not sure, but nice to meet you. You look familiar."

The conversations were going nowhere.

"What should we name them?" Tomo asked Mithra.

"I don't know," Mithra said. "I think we should let Jasper name them."

"Oh," Jasper said, straining under his decision. "I think I'll call them Jasper One, Jasper Two, Jasper Three…"

Jasper pointed at a different snowman each time he said a name. The elves looked at each other and began to laugh.

"There are names other than Jasper," one elf commented.
"Why don't we take them to the North Pole library?" another elf suggested. "They can pick their own names by finding something that interests them."

"We can leave the windows and doors open so no one melts. It's going to be very cold tonight," added a third elf.

Jasper loved the idea. The snowmen followed the elves to the library while Mithra and Tomo returned to meet the team for dinner. Jasper had high expectations that each one of them would find a particular interest and name themselves accordingly. He was so excited that little flakes of snow stood up on his arm.

16

The next morning, at 6 o'clock, Ben woke everyone up and instructed them to get dressed. This was their first morning of stretching and exercise. The team put on their warm base layers and started their routine. Ben could tell that Tiberius, Tomo, and Nebo were used to physical activities. Mithra was giving it her best shot. Gus went through the motions, but was not really stretching out much. Josef was a problem.

Josef had never done anything physical without being forced to do so. He was repulsed by the idea of working out. While the others were actively stretching, he was nonchalantly lying on his back. Ben was annoyed by this lack of effort, but determined to have the whole group train together.

Ben slowly approached Josef. "You can do this Josef, please try to raise your leg to your chest."

Reluctantly, Josef raised his leg a few inches off the ground and grabbed his knee. It required a considerable exertion on his part to do this limited movement. He repeated with the other leg. Ben focused his attention on Josef for the next hour and by the end, Josef seemed to loosen up a bit and gain some confidence.

"Go ahead and stand now Josef," Ben requested.

Josef stood up quickly. He smiled and looked at Ben. He felt energized. Not only that, the act of standing was not as tedious as it usually was.

"That was easy," Josef commented.

For the first time in his life, Josef felt his body working. He took a few steps to test his legs out. The stretching routine Ben had guided him through made Josef aware of his body. Up to this point, he had only focused on the effort and pain his movements created.

"I feel good," Josef said with a sense of surprise. "I like this stretching, it makes standing and walking easier."

Ben only felt pity for the large boy. No one had ever taken the time to help him understand his body. Ben knew his own perfectly, he knew his strengths and weaknesses. More importantly, he knew exactly what he could and could not do physically. He was excited to help Josef realize his own potential.

At seven o'clock, the kids sat down to breakfast. Mithra and Tomo amused the group with the story of the snowmen waking into consciousness. They all wondered how the naming project in the library had turned out.

"I think they will be named after animals," Gus said.

"I bet they'll find the periodic table of elements and name themselves after atoms," Mithra mused.

"I hope they chose military leaders from history," Ben added. "It would be cool to have Napoleon, Washington, Genghis Khan, Alexander the Great..."

"I doubt it," Tomo interrupted. "When we last saw Jasper, he was going to call them Jasper 1, Jasper 2, and so on."

The kids erupted in laughter. Tiberius had a big smile on his face. He could really see the team starting to loosen up and come together. He was looking forward to the specialized training they were going to do next to help strengthen their bond further.

"What are you and Tomo planning for us after breakfast?" Tiberius asked Ben.

"Snowball fight!" Ben answered.

They finished breakfast as quickly as possible and were dressed and outside before eight o'clock. As Ben was dividing the group into two squads, Jasper and the snowmen strolled up.

"So what did you guys come up with last night?" Mithra asked eagerly.

"We spent most of the night looking at star charts," Jasper answered. "Some of these snowmen have recollections of a frozen world so we looked through different charts and each picked the name of an astronomical body."

"Over there are the ones named after the planets: Mercury, Venus, Earth, Mars, Jupiter, Saturn, Uranus, Neptune, and Pluto." Jasper pointed to his left. "The rest are named after stars, galaxies, comets, and constellations."

"Impressive," Mithra said approvingly.

Ben jumped in with a spontaneous idea. "Hey, how would you guys like to have a snowball fight with us? We were going to have one amongst ourselves but it would be better if all of you were involved. You think you're ready for that?"

"Yes!" replied the newly formed universe of snowmen.

"Great! Let's take twenty minutes to get ready," Ben suggested. "Then we can begin the fun."

The kids looked at Ben. Everyone, except Nebo, looked worried.

"I don't really like snowball fights," Gus complained. "It's one thing to have a few kids throwing snowballs at each other but taking on fifty-one snowmen seems impossible."

"If we work together we can win this," Ben said confidently. "Come on, guys. It will be fun. Besides, everyone, except Jasper, is only one day old."

Nebo and Mithra laughed at the joke, but the rest of the group did not appreciate the humor. With the exception of

Ben, none of the kids had ever been a part of a team effort before. They were used to working alone and did not know how a team was supposed to function. Ben knew otherwise.

Ben instructed them on how to prepare. Some joined together to roll a bunch of giant snowballs to use in constructing a defensive fortress. Ben noticed Nebo had incredible strength. He had the power to roll humongous snowballs within a short time. Toward the end of his snowball creation, he resembled a dung beetle pushing a giant, round object.

Josef was not so strong. He sat in the same place and listlessly rolled a number of small snowballs to be used for throwing. Mithra and Gus also focused on forming snowballs to be thrown. Tiberius and Tomo worked on filling in the gaps left between the big snowballs in the structure of the fortress.

The fifty-one snowmen simply watched in amusement. A few would occasionally roll a snowball and throw it randomly, but they were not preparing at all. They were confident superior numbers would be the deciding factor.

"Ben, I think there is a way to stop them quickly," Mithra said. "There's a limit to the size of the snowmen. If we get enough snow to attach to each of them, they'll slow down and eventually stop moving."

"Perfect," Ben responded. "Great plan."

"Ready to go?" Ben shouted from behind the fortress.

The walls were seven feet high and twenty feet long. It was shaped like the letter "C". Inside were hundreds of preformed snowballs.

The snowmen formed into a single long line spread out before the fortress. Jasper took the role of leader and settled behind the others in order to shout instructions.

"Forward march!" he commanded the frozen squad.

"Don't throw snowballs until you're sure you will hit them," Ben yelled.

Josef had been on the losing end of quite a few snowball fights and did not like the odds of this one. Everyone shared his trepidation as the snowmen approached.

"Now!" Ben shouted.

Most of the kids summoned the courage to stand up from behind the wall and launch a barrage of snowballs toward their intended target. The snowmen were taking heavy hits and paused to regroup and scoop up snow. Soon, snowballs were flying in both directions.

"Hit the closest ones," Ben ordered.

The team reacted well to Ben's command. Tomo scored precise hits. Although Tiberius could throw fast, he had poor aim. Josef and Gus cowered behind the wall.

"They're getting closer," Mithra called down to Josef. "We need to launch a bigger offensive. We need your help, Josef."

Josef heard her plea and froze for a moment. He was surprised that *he* was being asked to help win the fight. He mustered as much courage as he could and looked over the parapet of the fortress. Some of the snowmen seemed to be frozen but dozens more were getting close to the snow fortress. His companions were throwing as fast as they could.

Somewhere deep inside Josef a strength rose up. He recalled snowball fights with kids from school. It often ended with the whole school attacking him. But no matter how many came at Josef, he was always able to return a few well-aimed shots. He did not win those snowball fights, but he did enough to deter his assailants and eventually he was left alone. He had thrown snowballs before. He could do it again.

He determinedly climbed over the top of the wall and began his own swift throws. His aim was perfect. He hit the closest snowman flawlessly and rapidly. Soon the target was frozen. He switched to the next snowman and had a similar result. In a short time, it was evident to all that Josef was actually the most effective hurler.